The Author

served as Ambassador to Spain from 1933 to 1937 and then became Ambassador to Chile until his retirement last year. Among the best known of his books are *The Tragic Era, Party Battles of the Jackson Period, The Young Jefferson, Jefferson and Hamilton, Jefferson in Power,* and the recently published *My Mission to Spain.* Mr. Bowers delivered these four essays as the 1953 J. P. Young Lectures in American History at Memphis State College.

THE J. P. YOUNG LECTURES IN AMERICAN HISTORY
Memphis State College, Memphis, Tennessee

MAKING DEMOCRACY A REALITY

Making Democracy A Reality

Jefferson, Jackson, and Polk

By
CLAUDE G. BOWERS

MEMPHIS STATE COLLEGE PRESS
MEMPHIS
1954

Library of Congress
Catalog Card No. 54-11630

FIRST EDITION

Manufactured in the U. S. A.
By the McCowat-Mercer Press, Inc.
Jackson, Tennessee

Introduction

Within the pages of this volume is found a lucid statement of the beliefs of Claude G. Bowers concerning Thomas Jefferson, James K. Polk, and Andrew Jackson. Sufficient it is to say that Mr. Bowers, himself an ardent disciple of Jefferson and Jackson, reaffirms his faith in their teachings and his loyalty to his great preceptors.

Mr. Bowers has given to readers of American history three distinguished volumes relating to the monumental work of Thomas Jefferson in founding the American concept of democracy. From his pen has also come the noteworthy *Party Battles of the Jackson Period,* portraying with devoted sincerity the epic battles of Old Hickory to maintain the influence of the common people in the affairs of government.

The present volume embraces those characteristics which inspired William G. McAdoo to write: "With keen-sighted scholarship and in facile style he has achieved a volume of admirable historical quality, worthy to rank with the finest presentations of men and events." William E. Dodd, eminent American historian, pronounced Mr. Bowers the author of the most interesting book ever written on the struggle between Jefferson and Hamilton. The essays contained in the following pages maintain the rich traditions of Mr. Bowers' distinctive prose style. More important, these timely lectures present a strong reaffirmation of the author's abiding faith in democratic processes. The democracy of Claude G. Bowers is as consecrated as it can be, and his honesty and sincerity match his devotion to democracy.

James K. Polk emerges as a positive force in the fight for democracy and as a great contributor to the acquisition of the Mexican Cession. Polk has long merited the attention of an historian of the caliber of Claude G. Bowers, and here is recognition adequate for the moment, an essay worthy of becoming a biography. Bowers places Polk on the national scene in the company of great statesmen and consummate politicians; he gives in this lecture the best picture of Polk presently available.

The establishment and publication of the J. P. Young Lectures in American History is made possible through a grant from the Herbert Herff Foundation. The publication of these lectures has been furthered by valuable assistance from the Henry and Lena Meyer Kahn Trust. The Memphis State College Press is possible only through the assistance of the above-named foundations.

Appreciation is due to Mr. Abe D. Waldauer for constant encouragement and help in establishing the lectureship and in making the Memphis State College Press a reality.

Lee N. Newcomer has served as editor of the volume. Appreciation is hereby expressed to Mr. Newcomer and his colleagues on the history staff for much hard work and sound advice. We are grateful also to Mrs. D. C. Sossomon for typing and for other valuable assistance.

July 1, 1954 Enoch L. Mitchell

CONTENTS

1

THOMAS JEFFERSON

His Final and Decisive Struggle for American Democracy

I

IN THESE DAYS of shifting values the democratic concept of society is being challenged on two fronts. On the one there are the communists and on the other the fascists, and these two are as one in their common purpose to exterminate democracy, to destroy the freedoms, and to make man a mere cog in the machine of a police state. These two despotic systems are all too successful in creating the impression that one must subscribe to one or the other. As much as sixteen years ago democracy was shoved on a sidetrack, and the gravest portent of the times was the ease with which presumably intelligent people were persuaded that one had to be a communist or a fascist.

Long ago, Lord Macaulay predicted the disintegration of American democracy on the ground that a Babel of contradictory forces would arise to confuse the popular mind. Never in America's long national story has this prediction seemed so ominous. Never has the need been greater to review and reappraise the democratic or the American way of life, and for the generality of people to familiarize themselves with the processes and the struggles through which we established the governmental system and adopted the philosophy through which we have made phenomenal progress and become the most powerful nation on the earth in which men are free.

It is commonly said by historians that the Americans of colonial days were instinctively democratic, and that is true; that before landing from the *Mayflower* the Pilgrim Fathers agreed upon a democratic system, and that is true. They who broke with their past in Europe to brave the dangers of the wilderness came here to regain the freedoms of which they had been deprived. They came in search of the liberties compatible with the dignity of man. They came to worship God according to the dictates of their conscience. They came that they might think aloud without fear of spies, punishment, or prison. Yes, it is true that the mass of the people in colonial days were instinctively democratic, but it is a mockery of history to assume from this that the democratic instinct reached a great portion on the higher level from which sprang the leaders of the people. No, democracy came to America in its institutions only after a prolonged and bitter struggle and when a leader worthy of the democratic cause appeared upon the scene in Thomas Jefferson.

Here was a man of property, of the aristocracy of blood and brain, partial to gracious living and beautiful surroundings, and the aristocracy or the oligarchy of his youth could not understand his renunciation of the creed of his class. He was denounced by these as a renegade in his time, and we hear echoes of that denunciation to this day. His father was of pioneer stock, a self-made man, and through his mother's veins coursed the aristocratic blood of the Randolphs. From his father he inherited his political democracy, and from his mother, his concept of gracious living. Though he admits that during his first year in college he frequented the company of horse racers, cardplayers, fox hunters, and roisterers, squandering his money in gambling and in other barren ways, he soon settled down to such intensive studies that he scarcely had time for physical exercise. His remarkable maturity at college is manifest in the fact that at eighteen he became the boon companion of the royal governor, Francis Fauquier. This man, then old, and with high culture and experience in public life, had been equally at home in the highest society and the gambling clubs of London where his losses had condemned him to his exile in Virginia. In the drawing room of his palace young Jefferson came under the influence of William Small, a Scotch professor of philosophy, and George Wythe, a great lawyer and jurist who was equally in his element in politics and philosophy. Recalling the Attic evenings with these men, each old enough to be his father, Jefferson was to say that, "I have never heard more good sense, more rational and philosophic conversation in all my life beside." It was there in the Fauquier drawing room that he turned the plates of the works of Andrea Palladio, leader in the Italian architecture of the sixteenth century, which resulted in the rich flowering of Monticello.

In boyhood and youth in reading the pages of Addison, Steele, and Swift, he mastered the art of writing. He pored over the pages of Richardson, Fielding, Smollett, Sterne, and Cervantes though he was never an inveterate reader of fiction. His preference was for history and philosophy. He knew intimately the historians of the Greeks and Romans, and he mastered their philosophy as well. He studied the supreme orators of antiquity, and while he thought Demosthenes a greater orator than Cicero, he found Cicero a greater philosopher than Socrates. He was familiar with the works of Shakespeare, Milton, Pope, Dante, and Molière.

More interesting in the evaluation of his political character was his absorption in political philosophy. His detractors, getting their cue from the hostile propagandists of the days of his preeminence, have pretended to trace his democracy to

Voltaire and Rousseau, but there is nothing in his writings to indicate that either had the slightest effect upon his thinking. If he was influenced in his thinking by the philosophers of the eighteenth century, it was by the Englishmen, John Locke and Lord Kames. For a time he was impressed by Montesquieu's *Spirit of the Laws,* but later he was to challenge many of its conclusions.

No one, perhaps, had a more determining influence in the molding of his political character than George Wythe under whom he studied law. His preceptor was a lawyer of erudition, a great jurist, an original thinker in political science, and a philosopher who believed in the democratic concept of society. In the office and the home of this great man the conversation turned to history, philosophy, and the wrongs suffered by the colonies. By the time Jefferson had reached his majority, few men in Virginia were so widely read and none was a greater master of the written word. Even this early he envisioned a society of freemen, and, subconsciously perhaps, he had dedicated his genius to the struggle for democracy in America.

Though the most consummate politician in our history, he was primarily a political philosopher with no desire for political preferment. Reading his voluminous correspondence it is clear that his conception of a happy life was that of a planter supervising his plantation, tending to his peas and potatoes, his flowers and shrubbery, corresponding with scientists and scholars, reading and conversing with men of culture on government, science, and political philosophy, and meditating on the trend of the times in the serene surroundings of his loved Monticello.

II

That a young man of his rare attainments and class should be sent to the House of Burgesses was inevitable. Never in

American history has there been a more brilliant group assembled in a legislative body than that in which the young planter in his twenties now found himself. There was Washington and Patrick Henry, George Wythe and Edmund Pendleton, Richard Henry Lee and Benjamin Harrison, Peyton Randolph and Richard Bland, each and every one a master in statecraft; and among these the tall red-haired youth was recognized as an equal of rare political potentialities. He moved among them with his usual modesty of demeanor. In the controversy with the mad monarch of Windsor this assembly was divided into militants and appeasers, and Jefferson took his stand with Patrick Henry and Richard Henry Lee.

It was here that young Jefferson emerged from the mass to take his rightful place as the penman and philosopher of the Revolution. The legislature was engaged in framing instructions to the Virginia delegation in the Continental Congress. Jefferson had found nothing inspiring or definitive in the protests and petitions sent to London. To him they seemed superficial, and he had delved deep. He sat down on his hill to put his thoughts on paper. The usual thought was of reforms, graciously granted; he thought in terms of a new society. Finishing his manuscript he began the long, dusty drive to Williamsburg, but, overcome by illness on the way, he returned to Monticello. The manuscript was sent on to the capital and laid upon the table for inspection.

When it arrived, the instructions had been already agreed upon after long deliberation, and it seemed too late to reopen the discussion and much too late for the consideration of a manuscript as iconoclastic, as exhaustive, and profound. But it made such a deep impression on Peyton Randolph that he invited the leaders to hear it read by him. The company sat in silence listening to an exposition of American rights that challenged the thinking of many generations. It was agreed that it should be published in pamphlet form and given a wide circulation. When it reached the members of the Continental Congress it was read with amazement and delight, and its author was instantly recognized as a genius of the highest order. When the pamphlet reached London, it made such an impression on the great orator, statesman, and philosopher, Edmund Burke, that he made a few alterations to make it more palatable to English taste; and it was published as a pamphlet in England by the party in opposition to the policies of the monarch, and it ran into several editions.

This unique pamphlet, known as a *Summary View of the Rights of British America,* set forth with unusual force the grievances against the mother country, as others had done, but it also foreshadowed Jefferson's political creed. It submitted that the people who migrated to the colonies had a right to establish "new societies," and that truly revolutionary claim was something novel in the struggle for national independence. It was democratic. It challenged the feudal system as to land by denying the king's dominion over the soil and his right to parcel it out among his favorites—and this foreshadowed his fight against, and his destruction of, the laws of primogeniture and entail.

Jefferson himself said that his document was "thought too strong for the times" and that "if it had any merit, it was that of first taking our true ground, and that which was afterwards assumed and maintained."

It is not surprising that when, a little later, Lord North presented his Conciliatory Resolution, conceived in trickery, with no real conciliation or concession, young Jefferson was called upon to phrase the reply; and so powerful was the answer, and so happily phrased, that the Continental Congress adopted it as its own.

III

Thus, when this young man of thirty-two entered the Continental Congress, he was preceded by the reputation of a political genius of a high order with a special facility in the phrasing of a philosophy. When at length the futility of bombarding London with pleas and petitions convinced the Congress that the hour for separation from the mother country had struck, it is not surprising that young Jefferson should have been made a member of the small committee to frame the Declaration of Independence. It *is* remarkable, however, that Jefferson received more votes than John Adams or Benjamin Franklin who had long been conspicuous in the public service; and even more remarkable that despite his youth, he should have been unanimously chosen to phrase the historic document. It is not remarkable that Jefferson, modest and deferential to his elders, should have proposed and urged that the task be assigned to Adams. But in view of his vanity, it *is* remarkable that Adams should have declined the honor and insisted on Jefferson's acceptance. We have Adams' own version. He thought it politic that the framer of the Declaration should be a Virginian. He said that he had enemies due to his brusque clashes with his colleagues, and that Jefferson had none. More determining, perhaps, was his observation that Jefferson "had the reputation of a masterly pen, and been chosen a delegate from Virginia in consequence of a very handsome public paper . . . which had given him the reputation of a fine writer."

In the *Letters of Members of the Continental Congress* we have an intimate description of these two great men at the moment of decision. Jefferson had asked Adams to phrase the Declaration.

"I will not," said Adams.

"You should do it," insisted Jefferson.

"Oh, no!"

"Why?" Jefferson insisted.

"Reasons enough," said Adams.

"What can be your reasons?" asked Jefferson.

"Reason first, you are a Virginian and a Virginian ought to appear at the head of this business. Reason second, I am obnoxious, suspected, and unpopular. You are very much otherwise. Reason third, you can write ten times better than I can."

And so it came to pass that Jefferson sat down one hot day in his modest apartment in the Shippen house, at the desk he had himself designed, to write one of the most famous public documents the world has known. He had no books about him. He wrote rapidly out of the fullness of his knowledge, and within two days the document was finished. His long arraignment of the injustice of the British government was eloquent and devastating, but today it has only an academic interest. To this portion only did the committee and the Congress propose some alterations. It does not appear that the preamble, which alone had major meaning, surpassing all the rest in significance, attracted congressional attention. But in this preamble was condensed the spirit of the generality of the people, and here we have the proclamation of America's adherence to the principles and philosophy of democracy. It contained no new thought. It was merely a restatement of the most popular belief. But for the first time in a national assembly, the people, as a people, had declared that governments derive "their just powers from the consent of the governed"; that all men are "created equal"—which means equal before the law; that they are "endowed by their Creator with certain unalienable Rights, that among these are Life, Liberty and the pursuit of Happiness"; and that the people may change their government if necessary to maintain these inalienable rights.

The early future was to show that not a few who accepted that declaration did not believe in democracy at all. Jefferson did.

IV

Among the men who supported the Revolution, there was not a common purpose. Among the leaders the purpose of many was to get rid of onerous taxation without representation; some saw in the Revolution a mere change in rulers; and there were a few who felt with Jefferson that the opportunity was presented for the creation of a new society, foretold by him as a right in his *Summary View.*

That all too few thought as he thought was impressed upon him by the promulgation of a new constitution in Virginia. There was little in this to indicate a trend toward political and social progress since it embodied the spirit of reaction. It was not democratic in content and it was antidemocratic in the method of its adoption. It had not been written by men elected by the people for the purpose. It had not been submitted to the people for ratification or rejection. Meditating on the reactionary trend in Virginia, he who had just attained immortality in the writing of the Declaration of Independence was far from happy. He voluntarily retired from Congress, put on the armor of battle for the realization of his democratic society, and returned to the legislature to lead in the struggle for democratic reforms.

Within four days after taking his seat he had struck a deadly blow at the lingering feudalism of his native state. When he presented his bill providing that tenants entail should hold their lands in fee simple, he struck at the root of the oligarchy based on the landed aristocracy. The old system, borrowed from that of William the Conqueror in England, had as its purpose the perpetuation of wealth in favored families, and that was the antithesis of democracy. This battle, bitter but brief, was won, and a pillar of feudalism fell.

The destruction of the law of primogeniture—likewise devised for the perpetuation of wealth in favored families—followed quickly. Jefferson saw neither reason nor justice in denying the father the right to distribute his property among his children as he saw fit; and least of all did he, the father of adored daughters, see any decency in the disinheritance of these. Thus, he was among the first stout champions of the rights of women. Another pillar of feudalism fell.

Striving for a democratic society, he knew that democracy cannot thrive on the ignorance of the mass of the people. He knew that laws will be wisely framed and honestly administered only when the average man is sufficiently educated to act intelligently in public matters. And Virginia offered no educational facilities for the sons and daughters of the masses. In a letter to Madison, Jefferson said, "Above all things I hope the education of the common people will be attended to; convinced that on their good sense we may rely with the most security for the preservation of a due degree of liberty."

The measure he presented, foreshadowing the public school system of today, was certainly revolutionary. The oligarchy of the aristocracy objected to being taxed for the education of the poor man's son. It feared the diffusion of knowledge among the people. Years were to intervene before the realization of Jefferson's dream of popular education. But ultimately the dream came true, and the little red schoolhouse for more than a century and a half has munitioned and armed the people for the defense of liberty and human rights. Tear down the schoolhouse or wreck it through miserly appropriations for the schools and colleges, and in a generation democracy would be a memory.

But Jefferson, wielding his ax and likewise building, was not yet through. He had the courage and the wisdom to present a bill for the separation of church and state. He did not believe that a civil functionary is the custodian of the conscience of the people, and he knew that the state church ministers were the eager allies of the old oligarchy—more politicians than preachers. In this struggle he encountered the most vicious opposition he ever was to meet, but in the end the separation of church and state was achieved.

That accomplished, he struck at the tyrannical, intolerant laws through which the Methodists, the Baptists, the Presbyterians, and the Quakers had been persecuted and proscribed. Their places of worship had been put beyond the pale; their congregations were dispersed by force; their ministers were dragged from the pulpit and thrown into jails like common felons; and while shame discouraged the enforcement of all these measures of religious intolerance, Madison was to witness scenes of incredible brutality. To guarantee religious liberty and the freedom of the conscience, Jefferson now appeared with his immortal Bill for Establishing Religious Freedom which dealt a fatal blow at religious tyranny and intolerance, and again he had to fight a bitter battle against the oligarchy, which finally was won. In this he proclaimed the freedom of the human spirit and demolished all laws that stood between a man's conscience and his God. That document is one of the noblest ever penned by the hand of man.

Because of this bill he was to be deluged with slander, bespattered with slime throughout his life, and denounced as an atheist, a scoffer at Christ—he who demolished all legal barriers that made it a crime for Christians to subscribe to the creed of their choice.

The battles he fought in Virginia for a functional democracy were the most conclusive in American history.

V

In Jefferson's fight for democracy and the freedoms, a few years intervened between his labors in the legislature and his years as a diplomat in Paris. This interval was one of shadows and sorrow. The death of the wife he loved left him prostrate for weeks, and in the seclusion of his study in Monticello he wrote his one important book, *Notes on Virginia,* which deserves a careful reading by all who would understand his philosophy. His years in Paris were, perhaps, the happiest of his life in public station. Conversing with philosophers and scholars, with scientists and artists, meandering among the bookstalls on the Seine, inspecting new inventions, enjoying the companionship of charming women—and delighting in their company—he was ideally situated to observe at close hand the political ferment at the beginning of the French Revolution. His detractors among historians have sought to associate him with the demagogues who later plunged the country into a welter of blood in the Reign of Terror, but these men were still obscure and unknown to him when he was in Paris. He did have contact with the sane and moderate leaders, with men like Lafayette, Barnave, and Lameth. Hailing with delight the upsurgence of the democratic spirit and the destruction of feudalism, he discussed with these enlightened men the trend of the times and the problems of the hour in his house on the Champs Elysées. His advice was asked and given. The monarchy, under the heavy burden of its tyrannies and crimes, its extravagance and contempt for human rights, was trembling to its fall. The French statesmen with whom he conferred hoped to wipe out the old despotic forms and establish a democracy, dedicated to liberty and the rights of man under a constitutional system and the leadership of the king.

With this in view Jefferson proposed a plan that might have saved the monarchy by making the government responsive to the needs and demands of the people. With his own hand he wrote a bill of rights. In sending it to one of his familiar conferees he urged "most strenuously an immediate compromise to secure what the Government was now ready to yield, and trust to future occasions for what might still be wanting." It was the concept of a great statesman. He proposed that the king, in royal séance, "should come forward with a charter of rights in his hand to be signed by himself and every member of the three orders"; and he predicted that the patriots would carry back to their constituents "more good than ever was offered before without violence." What he proposed was that the king should place himself at the head of the Revolution.

And what was this bill of rights? The States-General should assemble without call and remain in session at its pleasure; the lawmakers alone could levy taxes and themselves determine the expenditure of the public funds. The old despotic practice of throwing men into the Bastille at the pleasure of the monarch or his toadies, without a charge, without a trial, and with no terminal facilities for their ultimate release, should end, and no one "should be restrained of his liberty but by regular process from a court of justice"; anyone otherwise restrained should have recourse to the writ of habeas corpus. The military establishment should be subordinate to the civil authorities. The press was to enjoy all freedom but be subject to prosecution for libel. The pecuniary privileges and exemptions enjoyed for generations by the parasites of the nobility would be denied.

Had Louis XVI had the courage and character to have appeared dramatically before his people with this charter in his hand, a democracy would have been possible without recourse to the unspeakable crimes that were to stain the Revolution.

Here again is the philosophy of Jefferson in condensed form.

VI

It was just at this moment, with Jefferson's mind fixed on a bill of rights, that a copy of the Constitution of the United States was placed on his desk. He read it with amazement. He had no fault to find with the provisions intended for the creation of a stable government, but he was shocked by the absence of one line for the protection of the people against the abuse of power. He had just proposed a bill of rights for the French, and his own people had failed to give it to the Americans. Had he at that time had the opportunity to read the debates in the Constitutional Convention he would have found an ever recurring distrust of democracy. It was not covert, it was open. Soon he was to learn that a bill of rights had been proposed; that Alexander Hamilton, who hated democracy, had opposed its incorporation as unnecessary; and that his own disciple, James Madison, had concurred. This aroused his indignation, and in a letter to Madison, approving the Constitution as a whole, he said there was one thing he did not like: "I will now tell you what I do not like. First, the omission of a bill of rights, providing clearly, and without the aid of sophism, for freedom of religion, freedom of the press, protection against standing armies, restriction of monopolies, the eternal and unremitting force of the habeas corpus laws, and trials by jury in all matters of fact triable by the laws of the land, and not by the laws of nations."

And then, clearly nettled by Madison's letter setting forth Hamilton's theory that the rights of the people could be assumed, he spoke sharply: "Let me add, that a bill of rights is what the people are entitled to against every government on earth, general or particular, and what no just government should refuse, or rest on inference."

Thoroughly aroused, his pen flew over the paper in letters to Washington, Madison, Monroe, and Giles protesting against the absence of a bill of rights as a protection against arbitrary governmental action by either the executive or legislative branch. To Washington he expressed the hope for the "annexation of a Bill of Rights" since it would "remove the danger of the opposition to the residue." This, he added, could be done by Congress "without calling a convention which might endanger the most valuable parts of the system."

The rest is history. In the first Congress, Madison presented the first ten amendments to the Constitution which constitutes the Bill of Rights. We can alter the Constitution as to other features, but with the elimination or emasculation of the Bill of Rights, the American republic would cease to be a democracy and the liberties of the people would be without a guarantee. Thus, he who wrote the Declaration of Independence and the Bill for Establishing Religious Freedom successfully insisted on the Bill of Rights.

VII

Unhappily for him, Jefferson was summoned home by Washington to become the head of the cabinet as Secretary of State. In New York and Philadelphia he was startled by the tone in social and business circles. He found an embryo aristocracy, vocal and arrogant. In the higher social circles there was a snobbish craving for a court. Not a few would have established a monarchy with Washington as king but for the patriotism and common sense of that colossal figure. In the fashionable drawing room of the William Binghams in Philadelphia, presided over by the beautiful Mrs. Bingham who had lingered long with the courts of London and Paris, he found a contemptuous hostility to democracy and the rights of the common people; and there, over the wine and walnuts, the brilliant leaders of the party in power aimed barbs of wit at popular rights. In business circles he found the conviction that it was proper and wise to use the instrumentalities of government for the enrichment of the few. It was at this time that Hamilton was writing Robert Morris that to create a strong government it should be made profitable to the powerful. His hatred of democracy was inherent and it persisted to his death. He confided to Washington his contempt for public opinion. He had no interest in the worker in the factory or the farmer at the plow. He once described the people as "a great beast." He called the Constitution a "frail and worthless fabric," and he had no faith in it or in republican institutions. He was honest in his opinions, and he would resent any other interpretation of his political and social views.

This said, much may be added to explain the genius and the power of Hamilton. He was a genius of a very high order, a master in polemics, a brilliant expounder, a master of statecraft though not of politics, a natural leader and organizer of men, a great writer and orator, and an absolutely honest and courageous man. If he was involved in scandal, it was not that of money but of women, of whom he was a wee bit too fond. But he was not a typical American of his time. Though born in the West Indies, his political roots were in Europe.

Never in American history have there been antagonists remotely approaching Hamilton and Jefferson. To understand these two men is to comprehend the two eternal schools of political thought that they embodied. Hamilton was the most powerful enemy of democracy the nation has produced; and Jefferson was the greatest champion of democracy in American history. These two men could never have dwelt in harmony under the same tent and their presence in the cabinet of Washington made conflict inevitable.

On his return from Europe Jefferson found a powerful party under the leadership of Hamilton thoroughly entrenched, and there was no other party. The Federalist party was extraordinarily brilliant in its leadership from Hamilton down, and it had rallied to its support the influential, organized, commercial and financial interests of the young nation. Aligned with Hamilton were parliamentarians of ability, orators of eloquence, and men of daring and audacity. The Federal and state courts were literally packed with open, intense partisans who did not hesitate to sit in party caucuses for the consideration of measures that might reasonably be expected to reach them for judicial action. They had a militant, unscrupulous press, indifferent to the truth, and soon Hamilton himself, undercover, was writing attacks on Jefferson in the papers. The conflict between the two reached the cabinet meetings and the quarrels became increasingly distasteful to Jefferson. He disliked and suspected Hamilton's national bank and his economic policies in general. But when he found his Federalist colleague attempting interference with the foreign policy which was exclusively his business, he submitted his resignation to Washington. Twice he resigned, only to yield to Washington's importunities that he remain, but at length he submitted his resignation in undeclinable form and retired to the more agreeable atmosphere of Monticello.

Thus far there had been no interference with the right of the people to determine their policies at the ballot box; thus far measures inimical to the public interest could be defeated at the polls; thus far controversial questions could be debated from the platform and in the press without the interference of those in power. But scarcely had Jefferson retired when the

Federalists, powerfully entrenched, brazenly fared forth for the purpose of crushing the democratic sentiment of the people through terroristic methods. They would throw into the scrap heap the Bill of Rights on which Jefferson had insisted.

VIII

The first open defiance of the Bill of Rights in outlawing the freedom of discussion took the form of an attack on the democratic clubs that were springing up all over the country to meet the challenge of the antidemocratic policies of the Federalists in power. The enemies of democracy and even of democratic institutions had reached the point where, at a public dinner, they drank toasts to the foes of popular government while the band played "God Save the King," and in the fashionable Belvedere Club in New York they drank a toast to "the annihilation of liberty."

The membership of the democratic clubs was composed of men ranging from the humblest mechanic in a Boston workshop to the great David Rittenhouse, philosopher and scientist, who was president of the Philosophical Society of Philadelphia. They were drawn together regardless of social differences by the threat to the liberty and the economic interests of the mass of men. Their purpose was to present an organized opposition to measures inimical to the interest of the common man. They turned the searchlight on the congressional scene in Philadelphia, and when the club of Rittenhouse declared that the citizen had the right to "regard with attention and discuss without fear the conduct of public servants," the declaration was denounced as "seditious."

When the club in Norfolk summoned the people to a courageous expression of their sentiments, the Federalists described the summons as sinister. With the aristocratic leaders of the caste system in New England, where the masses of the people were ignored, this organization of democratic forces reaching down to the despised common people was looked upon as an outrageous pretension of people of no importance to the right to participate in government matters.

Through these clubs the common people took on a political significance they had never had before. They dared to study measures pending in Congress; dared read the speeches of their representatives in Congress; dared form opinions on their merits; dared express them in the streets, in public forums, in the press, and at the fireside; dared assume the existence of a democracy; and dared evoke the Bill of Rights as the guarantee of their privilege to make their views articulate.

The indignation of the Federalists mounted, and the clubs were denounced as "subversive" because of their avowed purpose to influence public opinion. Jefferson rejoiced in this awakening of the civic conscience of the people. He believed that the people, given the facts, could be counted on to reach wise conclusions, and he wished them to inform themselves and vigorously to express their views. Hamilton shuddered at the thought that should these clubs continue, even the mechanic would get the absurd idea that he had a legitimate interest in public measures and affairs. He had a plan to crush these clubs in their incipiency.

On his advice and urging Washington committed the gravest blunder of his career and attacked the democratic clubs in his message to Congress. James Madison described this attack as an assault on the citadel of liberty and "an attack on the essential and constitutional rights of the citizen." Jefferson, at Monticello, read the attack with amazement and described it in a letter to Madison as "one of the most extraordinary acts of boldness of which we have seen so many." He thought it "wonderful indeed that the President should have permitted himself to be the organ of such an attack on the freedom of discussion, the freedom of writing and publishing." In a letter to William B. Giles he used plain language:

> The attempt which has been made to restrain the liberty of the citizens of meeting together, interchanging sentiments on what subjects they please, and stating their sentiments in the public papers has come upon us a full century earlier than I had expected. To demand that the censors of public measures should be given up to punishment is to renew the demand of the wolves in the fable that the sheep should give up their dogs as hostages of the peace, and confidence established between them.

If, cowering behind the majestic figure of Washington, the Federalists thought to intimidate the Jeffersonians into silence, they were instantly disillusioned. The Federalists proposed to inject into the congressional reply to the President's message a special approval of the attack on the democratic clubs, but in the debate that ensued this met a brilliant and vigorous opposition. The crushing protests of Madison and Giles in unanswerable constitutional arguments, proclaiming the right of the citizen to scrutinize the conduct of public servants, to study and discuss public measures, and to express their opinions orally or in the press, and denouncing any interference as a brazen defiance of the Bill of Rights, gave pause to the Federalist plan. The reply went to the President without a reference to the attack on the processes of democracy.

But the attack had an intimidative effect, and the enemies of democracy won a partial victory in the desertion from the clubs of the timid.

This first attempt to reduce the Bill of Rights to a mockery is important since it was the prologue to the infamous attempt soon to be made to crush democracy under the heel of brutal might through the terroristic methods that were in incubation.

IX

It began with the determination of the Federalists to align the United States against their allies, the French; it approached success when a commission was sent to negotiate the differences with France, and Talleyrand, unquestionably on his own and in keeping with his character, demanded a bribe as a condition for negotiations; and it reached the climax with the appearance of the XYZ documents proving the truth of the charge. Then the war hawks launched their campaign of villification and misrepresentation to whip the people into a frenzy of fear and indignation. Used for party purposes, the batteries of abuse were turned upon the Jeffersonians and democrats. Mobs prowled the streets of Philadelphia attacking the house of Benjamin Franklin Bache, editor of the *Aurora,* smearing the statue of Franklin with mud from the gutters, and playing the "Rogue's March" beneath Jefferson's window. The Federalist spokesman in the House bowed low to Pitt with the assertion that all revolutions are the work of fools and knaves, philosophers and sans-culottes—a sentiment that could scarcely have been approved by Washington who had led a revolution of his own. The philosopher, of course, was Jefferson—also a fool and knave. Incredible as it seems that a state of hysteria should have been created for such flimsy reasons, it reached a point that startled Jefferson. When the excitement began to moderate, *Porcupine's Gazette,* the organ of William Cobbett, notorious on both sides of the Atlantic, announced under screaming headlines that the French army had landed in South Carolina and was marching northward burning plantation houses, kidnapping children, and raping women—and the hysteria mounted.

The atmosphere was just ripe for desperate measures definitively to put a period to democracy in America.

X

And then came the Alien and Sedition Acts.

The alien law was aimed, not at the few French in America, but at the Irish who had flocked in great numbers to the United States for refuge from the prisons and scaffolds when the rising of the United Irishmen was put down. It was natural that the greater part of the Irish refugees went to the Jeffersonians by instinct, partly because the philosophy of Jefferson conformed to their views, and partly because of the Federalists' blind devotion to England. That the alien law was aimed exclusively at the opposition is crystal clear, since the disreputable Porcupine, attacking Jefferson and Franklin with scurrility, was immune even though he was displaying pictures of George III and Lord North in his shopwindows. Many were demanding the application of the alien law to Albert Gallatin, the democratic leader born in Switzerland, and one of the greatest statesmen of the early republic. When Hamilton Rowan, a cultured Irishman, was threatened with arrest, Jefferson invited him to the refuge of Monticello with the assurance that in Virginia the writ of habeas corpus had not yet been suspended.

But the Federalists relied for their purpose more on the sedition law which was to crush the democratic aspirations of the people, tyrannize over the press and platform, and intimidate the Jeffersonians into silence. As first framed this law was so atrocious that it made friendship for France punishable by death, though we were not at war; so vicious that Hamilton protested on the ground that it would establish a tyranny. It was then modified without changing its tyrannical character.

The savage nature of the Federalist program was revealed during the congressional debate on the measure. When statesmen and patriots like Albert Gallatin and Edward Livingston could not be heard because of the coughing, laughing, talking, and scraping of feet on the floor, a representative democracy was being treated with cynical mockery. The Federalists could not afford to permit the people to hear the grave warnings of Livingston. His prediction, which soon was realized, is worth remembering even now:

> The country will swarm with informers, spies, delators and the odious reptile tribe that breeds in the sunshine of despotic power. . . . The hours of the most unsuspected confidence, the intimacies of friendship or the recesses of domestic retirement, afford no security. The companion whom you trust, the friend in whom you must confide, the domestic who waits on your chamber, are all tempted to betray your imprudent or unguarded follies; to misrepresent your words; to convey them distorted by calumny to the secret tribunals where jealousy presides, where fear officiates as censor, and suspicion is the only evidence that is heard. . . . Do not let us be absurd enough to call ourselves free and enlightened while we advocate principles that would have disgraced the age of Gothic tyranny.

The sedition, like the alien law, was passed by a narrow margin. Instantly the *Commercial Advertiser* of New York announced that any man who opposed the sedition law "deserves to be suspected"; the Hamiltonian editor, John Fenno, was immediately denouncing any criticism of the Adams administration as "treason"; and the fantastic theory was advanced that any member of Congress who attacked the sedition law on the floor should be numbered among the seditious. True, the leader of the Federalists, in a moment of gracious condescension, thought the chosen representatives of the people might attack the law on the floor, but publicity for the attack beyond the chamber should be subject to the sedition law. When a Virginia congressman, Samuel J. Cabell, dared write his constituents of the proceedings in Philadelphia, Judge Iredell, a Federalist politician on the United States Supreme Court, solemnly called it to the attention of the grand jury in Richmond. Indeed Federal judges, all fighting Federalists, were charging grand juries all over the country in favor of the sedition law and urging the punishment of its critics. Mobs were roaming over the land pulling down liberty poles; New England preachers, bearing false witness, were plumbing the depths of indecency with attacks on Jefferson and democracy. Eastern colleges, joining in the antidemocratic crusade, were lavishing honorary degrees on the crudest and least intellectual of Federalist politicians, while none went to Jefferson, president of the American Philosophical Society, author of the Declaration and the Bill for Establishing Religious Freedom, the friend of Franklin and Rittenhouse. The climax came when it was declared seditious to circulate petitions for the repeal of this nefarious law.

XI

During the congressional debates on the sedition law, Jefferson, presiding in the Senate, looked down with astonishment and abhorrence on the proceedings on the floor, although he presided over the disgraceful turmoil with dignity and restraint. He conferred daily with Madison, Gallatin, Livingston, and Giles on the strategy they were to follow. But the ruffians played the "Rogue's March" under his windows at night; his letters were illegally opened in search of a phrase that could be called "seditious," and the treacherous Timothy Pickering, Secretary of State, was feverishly reading Jefferson's papers to that end. Spies watched his house, dogged his footsteps, and penetrated to his table; preachers of New England circulated against him the bizarre lie that he was an atheist and had said that a dilapidated church was good enough for Him who was born in a manger; and Jefferson, the most cultivated man in the capital, was forced to avoid social gatherings since fashion hated democracy and was cheering the crimes against the freedom of the human spirit. He was so little perturbed by the personal attacks that in the midst of them he was writing letters to farmers on crop rotation and on a plow he had invented; and when he learned that a friend was making a journey beyond the Mississippi where wild horses roamed, he wrote him urging that he study these animals in their natural state and prepare a paper for the Philosophical Society.

While a consummate politician, Jefferson had no aspiration for public station. He had firmly refused to be a candidate for President in 1796, proposing that the honor be bestowed on Adams. He was even more political philosopher than politician. But as he surveyed the almost incredible scene he knew that all he believed in politically was under assault, and he entered the arena militantly in defense of the tenets of his political philosophy. With the war craze—born of misrepresentation and fear—mounting, John Adams, who craved popularity and seldom had it, delivered a provocative speech in denunciation of the French from the portico of his house while mobs swarmed into the street attacking democratic papers. The war hawks played on the fears of Adams, and when he received a warning from some mischievous wag that the democrats were about to burn down the town, he actually had the servants bear arms and ammunition through the back door, determined to die at his post. To the well-balanced mind of Jefferson this seemed insane. But when the war hawks declared hatred of the French a sacred duty, when the abuse of democrats in the churches drove them from their pews, when Federal judges were making war speeches from the bench, when Chief Justice Ellsworth of the Supreme Court in a charge to a grand jury made a ferocious attack on the democrats, Jefferson wrote that "there is no event, however atrocious, which may not now be expected."

The Terror had begun. Insulted in public, Jefferson pretended not to hear. When in Virginia he attended a small social gathering of his neighbors on Sunday the Federalist press declared this an "irrefutable proof of his contempt for the Christian religion," and because in his *Notes on Virginia* he had said that pebbles on the top of the Virginia mountains were not a proof of the universal flood, the political preachers again denounced him as an atheist.

In New York an unsavory mob attacked the home of Livingston and was put to flight by a company of fighting Irish. In Boston, Thomas Adams, distinguished editor of the *Chronicle,* was expelled from the Fire Society of which he had been a working member for fourteen years.

It was the darkest hour Jefferson was to know. When Congress met he directed his supporters to seek an adjournment to permit the members to consult their constituents. They tried and failed. When the two Federalist members of the commission to Paris returned to make the most of the XYZ papers for partisan ends, Elbridge Gerry, the Jeffersonian, remained behind, convinced that an amicable agreement could be reached. Jefferson, a strict disciplinarian in party matters, became impatient over his silence. He wrote Gerry that the people at home wished to know if his colleagues on the commission had acted like men seeking peace or an excuse for war, and that "your fellow citizens feel they have a right for full information." At length Gerry returned to Boston. During his absence, ruffians had tortured his wife and children by knocking on doors and windows, and had sent obscene letters to his wife saying that he had lingered in Paris because of a love affair. One day Gerry sat down with Adams in the house in Quincy and made a full report, and for the first time Adams, an honest man, awakened to the treachery of Pickering and his cabinet. This ended the XYZ scare.

But Jefferson knew that the voluminous report would not be seen by the average citizen. He wrote Edmund Pendleton to reduce it to a capitulation "stating everything, short, simple, and leveled to every capacity," and short enough to be printed on handbills to be posted on the walls. The philosopher was indeed a consummate politician.

XII

But with or without a French war as a pretext, the enemies of democracy were carrying on their reign of terror with the sedition law. For two years in these United States they were setting an example for the Hitlers and Stalins of a later generation. The crushing of the democratic spirit was to be accomplished through the persecution and suppression of the democratic press, the denial of free speech, and the practical blotting from the Constitution of the Bill of Rights. To visualize the infamy of the tyranny of those days it is worthwhile rapidly to touch on the crimes against liberty and human dignity when Jefferson assumed the leadership of the democratic forces.

For two years the Federalist press was full of reports on the arrest and imprisonment of democratic editors. Within the first few months after the sedition law went into effect, twenty-one editors had been arrested. One must go to the dark days of Jeffreys, the butcher in the reign of James II, to find a counterpart to the turpitude and shamelessness of the Federalist party judges in Federal courts. The reasons for the arrests were often fantastic and sometimes unthinkably absurd as in the case of the fun-loving wag who, on hearing the firing of a salute for Adams, laughingly said it was a pity the ball did not lodge in the seat of his pants. The harmless humorist was dragged into court for sedition.

Take the case of Matthew Lyon. He was a Revolutionary patriot and had fought with the Green Mountain Boys against the British. A convinced democrat and the editor of a newspaper, he concentrated his fire on the sedition law. In an article he had referred to Adams' "grasp for power" and his "unbounded thirst for ridiculous pomp," and that was "seditious." He was arrested and thrown into the most filthy jail that could be found in a tiny town, into a cell twelve by sixteen, with sanitary provisions unfit for the habitation of a dog, with iron-barred windows, and with his meager food passed through a hole in the door. He was refused pen and ink—for pen and ink had become instruments of sedition. When thousands signed a petition to Adams, he refused to receive it. Not content with the jail sentence, the court added a fine beyond Lyon's capacity to pay. The reaction of decent citizens came with his nomination and overwhelming election to Congress. When the time came for his release on the payment of the impossible fine, a Virginian rode into the village with the money in his saddlebags that Jefferson had helped to raise.

Take the case of Anthony Haswell, editor of the *Vermont Gazette,* a militant, democratic paper. In soliciting funds to pay the fine of Lyon he had referred to his "loathsome prison" and to the "hardhearted savage" who was his jailer, properly identified as a Tory during the Revolution. All this was true, but the truth had become seditious. Taken from his home at night in feeble health, he was forced to ride sixty miles to the capital on a cold night and in the rain. He was brutally refused dry clothing and he was thrown dripping wet into a cold cell in a wretched jail. A Federalist politician on the bench presided at the mockery of a trial, and he was found guilty of sedition.

Take the case of Thomas Adams, the great editor of the Boston *Independent Chronicle,* a militant champion of the Bill of Rights. When the Massachusetts legislature, predominantly Federalist, denounced the Kentucky and Virginia Resolutions and he made a devastating reply, he was arrested for sedition. He announced that the *Chronicle* would continue its fight and would "always support the rights of the people and the independence of the press." Too ill to be dragged into court, he announced from his sickbed that his paper would "stand or fall with the liberties of America and nothing shall silence its clarion voice but the destruction of every principle which leads to the achievement of our independence."

Furious because foiled momentarily by the illness of the editor, the Gestapo of the time arrested the bookkeeper for sedition on the ground that he had distributed the papers. The trial before Chief Justice Dana of Massachusetts was a shameless travesty of justice. The jurist on the bench, in the presence of the jury, bitterly attacked the lawyers for the defense as themselves guilty of sedition for daring to discharge their professional duty by defending an enemy of the sedition law. Not satisfied with this astonishing performance, he continued his attacks on the lawyers in the Federalist press. With such a judge on the bench and with a jury packed with partisans, as was the custom in all these sedition trials, the bookkeeper was found guilty. In sentencing the victim Dana exhausted the vocabulary of foul abuse on the lawyers for daring to "propagate principles" as "dangerous as those of the articles on which the indictment was based." This was so shocking that the *Chronicle* dared Dana to give his tirade to the press. The bookkeeper finally was thrown into a jail so miserable that public indignation forced a change. Day by day the paper went to press. With the editor sinking under disease and with the bookkeeper sick in jail, old Sam Adams, the patriot, stalked angrily to the jail, pounding the pavement with his stick to pay his tribute of admiration and adhesion. The bookkeeper served out his sentence, but within three days Thomas Adams was dead.

Take the case of Thomas Cooper, a distinguished English scientist and physician, but a friend of Jefferson. In an article he had criticized John Adams for negotiating a loan at six per cent in peacetime and with having invited a war by his intemperate attack on France which Jefferson thought the act of a madman. Presiding at his trial was Samuel Chase who had patterned his conduct on the bench on Jeffreys and Lord Clare. At the trial in the presence of a packed jury, he read and denounced the article in loud tones, and with savage observations Cooper was sentenced to jail for six months. When William Duane, a great editor, dared publish a report of the trial, the indignation of the Federalists knew no bounds. When a petition for Cooper's pardon was suggested, he rejected it on the ground that pardon should be preceded by repentance, and he was not repentant. "No," said Cooper, "I will not be a voluntary cat's-paw for electioneering purposes." The petition was dropped, and Cooper remained in jail with the consoling thought that his martyrdom was making enemies for the sedition law.

Take the case of James Callender, arrested for the publication of a pamphlet attacking the policies of the Adams administration. Again Chase presided, making violent attacks from the bench on the defendant and his lawyers. These lawyers, including the brilliant William Wirt, were distinguished at the Virginia bar. Constantly harassed and insulted by Chase they were refused permission to question witnesses. When one attempted an argument on the admissibility of evidence, Chase shouted an order to sit down. Storming, raving, threatening, he continued until the lawyers folded their papers and prepared to retire from the incredible mockery of the scene. When

Chase, now alarmed by his infamy, asked them to go on, they refused to continue the farce. Callender was found guilty of sedition and sent to jail.

Take the case of Charles Holt, editor of the New London *Bee.* Because he had denounced the unscrupulous propaganda to force us into a war with France, he was arrested for sedition. The paper on which the indictment was based had been furnished by two Federalist editors. One of them had two brothers on the jury that brought the indictment, and the foreman of the jury had been a commissary of the British army during the Revolution. When Holt was sentenced to jail for two months, a Federalist paper smugly commented on the "mildness of the punishment."

Take the pitiful case of David Brown. This simple old man had wandered about the countryside on his own, reading and passing out incomprehensible doggerel, and a Federalist leader as brilliant as Fisher Ames denounced him as an agent of Jefferson "set out to blow the trumpet of sedition." Just as dangerous as his doggerel was his participation in the raising of a liberty pole, inscribed with the sinister words, "No Stamp Act; No Sedition." Judge Chase presided at the trial. Solemnly he told the jury that the defendant was a critic of the Adams administration, that he had paid to have the inscription painted on the pole, and that he actually had held the ladder for the painter. He was sentenced to jail for a year and a half. Adams refused to receive petitions for his pardon. When the year and a half elapsed he had been forgotten, and he served two years before he was pardoned by Jefferson.

These cases illuminate the character of the crimes under the sedition law. But it not only was a crime to criticize public officials—it was seditious to circulate petitions for the repeal of the law. When John C. Ogden carried a petition for the release of Lyon, he was arrested for sedition. But more amazing is the case of Jedekiah Peck, a Federalist member of the New York legislature. Another Federalist, John Armstrong, distinguished author of the Newburgh Addresses that served the patriots' cause in the Revolution, prepared a powerful petition for the repeal of the sedition law and gave it to Peck for circulation. Peck was promptly arrested for sedition. Dragged from his bed at night, put in irons, thrown upon a horse, and accompanied by a cavalcade of armed Federalists not unlike the storm troopers of Hitler, he was paraded 200 miles in the rain to New York City. For five days the sorry procession passed through villages and towns, and the people looked upon the Federalist pageant with horror and disgust. It was a scene they would remember at the polls.

XIII

Meanwhile, with Pickering prying into the papers of Jefferson in search of a phrase on which he could be arrested for sedition, with the Federalist press denouncing him as a Maratist, a tool of Robespierre, an atheist, an anarchist, and a defender of assassination, Jefferson, who loomed mountain-high above such petty things, was intensely active. When democrats were fined, when democratic newspapers were suppressed, he was raising money to pay the fines and establish newspapers. He was writing down the names of friends with the contribution expected from each. He was directing the propaganda against the sedition law and advising his supporters in Congress. He was alarmed, not for himself, but for his country and the rights and liberties of freemen. He had radically differed with the Federalists on the bank and on some economic measures, but these measures did not alarm him. So long as the people were free to express their will at the polls, mistaken policies could be set aside. But now he was facing something that was elemental and went to the base of his democratic philosophy. Here was a program that would deprive the people of the right to rule themselves. As he reviewed the situation, he could not escape these facts: that the freedom of the press was being denied; that the freedom of speech was being made a crime; that the right of petition for the redress of grievances was being rejected; that the Bill of Rights on which he had insisted was being scrapped; that the democratic spirit of the people was being crushed beneath the brutal feet of might; and that the courts to which the people looked for the protection of personal and property rights were being converted into tribunals of injustice by partisan judges, presiding over packed juries and acting in accord with the dictates of party caucuses.

Here was a challenge to leadership that Jefferson had to accept. It was under these circumstances and for these reasons that he determined upon a dramatic challenge to arouse the fighting spirit of the nation and to reach the plain people in every quarter of the nation.

Conferring with such statesmen and patriots as Madison, Monroe, Gallatin, Giles, and Livingston, he reached a decision. He knew that the ultimate, inevitable result of a continuance of the tyranny would lead to the dissolution of the Union. Late in the summer of 1798 he sat down in a memorable conference on the lawn at Monticello with W. C. Nicholas of Virginia and John Breckinridge of Kentucky. Madison, unable to attend, had given his approval. The purpose was to reach the masses of the people through the legislatures of the various states. And out of the conference came the Kentucky and Virginia Resolutions declaring the sedition law unconstitutional and therefore null and void. Today, partly because of the battle Jefferson waged, the constitutionality of a law can be tested in the Supreme Court, but an appeal to the Court at that time, when the bench was packed with Federalist politicians, would have been a mockery.

These resolutions set forth the compact theory of the Union, but this did not enter into the debates in the legislatures. Jefferson made clear the justification for his audacious challenge when he wrote:

> If these laws should stand these conclusions will flow from them: that the general government may place any act they think proper on the list of crimes, can punish it themselves, whether enumerated or not enumerated by the Constitution or cognizable of them; that they may transfer its cognizance to the President or any other person who may himself be the accuser, counsel, judge and jury, and whose suspicion may be evidence, his order the sentence, his officer the executioner, and whose breast the sole record of the transaction. . . . unless the acts of tyranny be arrested on the threshold it would drive the States into revolution, furnish new calumnies against republican government, and new pretexts for those who wish it to be believed that men cannot be governed but by an iron rod.

He wrote Madison that the resolutions would support all vital principles but "leave the matter in such a train as that we may not be committed to push matters to extremities." The resolutions would be sent to the legislatures which would be asked to affirm that the sedition law was null and void.

And they served their purpose. In every legislature they were debated, and the debates, printed in the press, reached the people and put them on their guard. By taking the debate into every region, the people became intellectually cognizant of the threat to their rights and liberties. The debates themselves were debated in country stores, in the plowing field, and in the workshops, and discussed in the streets and about the firesides of the common people. Interest was aroused and intensified, and the issue raised proved to be the paramount issue in the approaching presidential election.

It mattered not that the Federalist legislatures refused to adopt the resolutions. That of Maryland refused them frankly because they called for the repeal of the Alien and Sedition Acts; that of Delaware because they were an interference with the plans of the general government. But the masses of the people were now munitioned, organized, and put on the march. They flocked to the polls in 1800 with the knowledge that they had it within their power to end a most brutal and audacious attempt to destroy the rights and liberties of men and to deny the democratic aspirations of the people.

Under the leadership of Jefferson the people were awakened to the threat to their liberties and civil rights, and he was borne triumphantly to the presidency. The Federalist party, contemptuous of democracy, indifferent to the common people and the rights of the ordinary man, was hurled from power, never to rise again. Historians have agreed that the election of 1800 definitively determined that ours should be a democratic republic. Thereafter, the press was free, freedom of speech was reestablished, and the courts ceased to be a shambles for the mutilation of human rights.

One day when Alexander von Humboldt, the great German scientist, was a guest at the White House, he found on Jefferson's table a scurrilous newspaper reeking with vicious attacks on his host. Utterly astounded, he turned to Jefferson to ask why such a paper was not suppressed and its editor sent to jail. Taking up the paper with a smile, Jefferson folded it and handed it to his guest. "Baron," he said, "if when you return to Europe any one there questions the freedom of the press in America, show them that paper, and tell them where you found it."

Every generation should know this story of Jefferson's struggle for democracy and meditate upon its meaning and take to the heart its warning. It is literally true, as a great philosopher has said, that those who forget the tyrannies of the past are condemned to experience them again.

XIV

The enemies of free institutions and the rights of the common man pursued Jefferson with their hatred for a full century after his death, and some historians have caricatured the greatest of Americans into our time. A lie runs fast and truth is hard pressed to overtake it. This universal genius now has the national memorial he so richly deserved. In Washington where so long he waited for a fitting monument now stands the beautiful memorial, majestic as his fame, to remind future ages of his greatness. No one can stand within this work of art, its walls adorned with his immortal utterances, in the impressive silence, without recalling with emotion the life of one of the greatest men in all the tide of time. Pictures flash before us—the young man at his homemade desk writing the Declaration of Independence; the valiant warrior of democracy wielding the ax at the feudalistic relics of Virginia; the statesman of world renown in Paris offering the king for his salvation a bill of rights he lacked the courage to accept; the militant champion of democracy, harassed by mobs and spies, assailed unceasingly with lies, yet unwavering in his faith in the sound sense of the people and storming the fortress of tyranny and unfurling above it the flag of all the freedoms for all time to come.

And in the solemn silence of the Jefferson Memorial other pictures come that bring him within the understanding of the average man. We see the farmer directing the sowing and the reaping and placing flowers and shrubbery; the lover of beauty creating Monticello and lovely houses for his friends; and the inventor fashioning plows, revolving tables, and laborsaving gadgets. We see him mothering his daughters and shopping for them in Paris, rummaging in the bookstalls on the Seine seeking treasures for his cronies, gossiping with philosophers and scientists, strolling in the Bois de Boulogne with Madame de Corny, and writing sentimental letters to Maria Cosway, the painter. We see him on his loved hilltop of Monticello, on the lawn with his neighbors enjoying as much as they the gossip of the neighborhood. We see him wherever he might be, fascinating his guests at the dinner table with the charm of his conversation, his exquisite tact, and his epicurean food and wines, and melting momentarily even the hostility of Gouverneur Morris. And we see him in the end, very old and feeble, watching the rising structures of the university he had designed for the training of leaders for the republic and tottering from his room to the dining room between rows of guests he did not know who came in a never-ending procession to do homage at the shrine of genius. He was a grand gentleman.

But within that memorial, so like a temple, the quotations from his pen inscribed upon the wall remind us that his immortality rests on his battles for a democracy blessed with all the freedoms, in which the lowliest man has rights that cannot be denied by a government of his choice.

2

JAMES K. POLK

Why Was He One of the Great American Presidents

I

JAMES K. POLK was born in Mecklenburg county, North Carolina, where his family had established itself before the Revolution. Tradition has it that the family had a part in the promulgation of the Mecklenburg Declaration of Independence, and his grandfather was an officer in the Revolution. His immediate family subscribed to the philosophy of Jefferson, and Polk himself never deviated one hairbreadth from the political principles of the father of American democracy.

In his eleventh year his father turned westward and settled in the valley of the Duck River in Tennessee which was then a wilderness. The health of the future President was not robust. His frame was not fitted for the strenuous labor that fell to the lot of the men who leveled the forests, drained the swamps, and followed the plow. Instead he cultivated his mind by assiduous studies. At a small academy near Columbia he "read the usual course of latin authors, part of the greek testament and a few of the dialogues of Lucian" as he recalled in later life. In his twentieth year he entered the University of North Carolina, dedicated himself intensively to his studies, and was graduated with the highest honors in mathematics and the classics. Returning to Tennessee, he began the study of law in the office of that truly great and brilliant Tennessean, Felix Grundy, with whom a close friendship was formed that continued without a break until the end. The record shows that he was highly successful at the bar. In his twenty-eighth year he was elected to the legislature, and the remainder of his life was given to the public service. It was at this time, when he urged the election of Andrew Jackson to the Senate, that his intimate association with the great man began.

II

Polk was in his thirtieth year when he was elected to the national House of Representatives. In those days of primitive travel he made his way on horseback over the miry roads to Washington where public men still lived simply. It is interesting to note that he messed with two men with whom in a few years he would be embroiled in controversy, John C. Calhoun and Hugh L. White. That he profited by his contact and conversation with these remarkable men one may take for granted.

Entering Congress during the administration of John Quincy Adams he aligned himself with the opposition. Making no pretense to eloquence, in no sense scintillating, he nevertheless impressed his colleagues in the arena of debate. He mastered his subject. He prepared himself by assiduous study. He had an orderly mind and he marshaled his facts and made them march. From the beginning he was one of the most versatile and powerful debaters in the House.

In the presidential campaign of 1828 he took an active part in the election of Jackson, and when the old hero of the Hermitage entered the White House, there was no one on the hill to whom the President looked with greater confidence; and from that hour on, only an illiterate, a moron, or a jaundiced partisan would ask the question, "Who is Polk?"

Never in American history have congressional battles been so bitter and brilliant as those that continued during the eight years of the Jackson administrations over the rechartering of the Bank of the United States and the removal of the deposits; and throughout these dramatic years the trusted leader and spokesman of the administration in the House was James K. Polk. The bank, through devious means, had mustered a comfortable majority of the members against Jackson, and among them were men of learning, of rare eloquence, and of parliamentary skill. In the Senate setting the pace and offering the shibboleths and battle cries, were such men of genius as Henry Clay, Daniel Webster, and John C. Calhoun. In the House the bank had dragged from lucrative practices some of the greatest lawyers of the American bar to defend its interests. With a safe majority in the House led by men of extraordinary ability and their views proclaimed to the public by a purchased press, the choice of a leader and spokesman of the administration was one of supreme importance.

In this leader and spokesman certain qualities were demanded. He had to have an exhaustive knowledge of the bank issue; he had to possess a clear and alert mind; he had to have sound judgment and an even temper to guard against the pitfalls of the enemy and against rash statements so easily uttered in the excitement of debate; he had to be a man of tireless industry; and he had to have the complete confidence of Jackson with whose views he had to have intimate knowledge. Naturally, he had to be absolutely loyal to his chief and to be a master of parliamentary procedure.

This leader, in the most bitter congressional battles ever fought, was found in James K. Polk. His record on the bank was unquestionable. Throughout his life he had accepted the view of Jefferson on the unconstitutionality of the institution conceived by Hamilton. He believed with Jackson that the bank was being used to further the economic and political interests of a class. And his intense loyalty to Jackson was unquestionable.

The bank had packed the strategic Committee on Ways and Means with its supporters including some of Jackson's party, and from this point of vantage, Polk, with the support of but two other members, went forth to battle when the committee launched an investigation of the institution. When the majority found the bank sound, the fight was on. Polk had made his usual exhaustive preparation for his speech. It was an argument clear as crystal, coldly logical, concise, closely knit, free from the abuse on which the enemy relied, and phrased with dignity. Thomas Hart Benton, in the Senate, wishing to make his indictment of the bank as impressive as possible, had drawn on his imagination for not a few of the alleged abuses that he enumerated, and the clever advocates of the bank discredited the whole by proving the absurdity of parts. Polk, in many respects a safer leader, made no such blunder. He rightly confined himself to charges that could be sustained. The power of his speech was immediately evident in the venom that was poured forth upon him and by the determination of the Whigs and their bank allies to defeat his reelection in Tennessee. Men as remote from Tennessee as Pennsylvania, New York, and Massachusetts interested themselves intensively in an effort to prevent his reelection. Fantastic lies were put in circulation. Had he not opposed pensions for Revolutionary soldiers? Was not an uncle of his a notorious Tory when Washington was fighting for our independence? Of course none of this was true, and he was triumphantly successful at the polls.

When he returned to Washington, the Jacksonians had a majority in the House, and Polk was made chairman of the

Committee on Ways and Means—the most important and powerful committee in the House, a post never given to men of small stature. Vitally important under normal conditions, it has never been more important than when, in 1833, Polk took over the chairmanship to lead the Jacksonians in their continuing war upon the bank.

This was renewed after Jackson had vetoed the recharter measure and had removed the deposits, and Roger Taney had submitted his report in justification of the act. This report was referred to the Committee on Ways and Means after a desperate attempt to have it otherwise handled. It was Polk who wrote the report justifying the removal of the deposits, and for two months a ferocious debate continued. The brilliant and fiery George McDuffie of South Carolina had made the principal speech in opposition; the reply was made by Polk. Again, as always was his custom, he was imposingly fortified with facts. Precedents and authorities he had at his tongue's tip. It was equally guarded against overstatement. Again, close reasoning and cold logic were so powerful that during the two months of debate that followed, every advocate of the bank concentrated on an effort to break down the argument of Polk.

Thus, with unerring judgment, he led the forces of the Jackson administration, and his leadership was acclaimed by the Jacksonians throughout the nation; but the Whigs and the minions of the bank poured forth their vials of wrath upon the leader they could abuse but could not overcome. And again the leaders of the Whigs and the bank, remote from Tennessee, did all within their power to defeat his reelection; and again he triumphed.

III

When Congress met again in December, 1835, he was elected speaker of the House of Representatives. There is no station in our government that demands and exacts higher qualities of leadership. The holder of this position has to deal directly with men of diverse temperaments, tastes, and sectional interests. Until recently the speaker named the committees and was potential in the molding of legislation. Petty men, without some rare qualities, never reach that rostrum.

Polk, whose gavel called the House to order, had for six years led in some of the most bitter struggles in American history. With not a few, the success of his leadership was a provocation. He ascended the rostrum in a period of extraordinary turmoil and sectional controversy. The bank minions, the nullifiers, and the abolitionists had reason to resent the courteous, impeccably dressed gentleman in the speaker's chair, and personal hate concentrated on an effort to make his task difficult. Because he followed the custom and gave his own party a majority on the committees, he was denounced as a tyrant. He was subjected to more heckling and insults than any of his predecessors because partisan hate fed on the memories of his effective leadership on the floor. Some of the insults were so indecent that his friends, including Jackson, were convinced that an attempt was being made to force him into a duel and to his death. Jackson advised him to ignore the attempt and to treat it and his traducers as beneath a gentleman's contempt, but his wife at one time feared for his life.

The Whigs put their heads together to concoct unusual and unprecedented questions to confuse him, but he was a master of parliamentary procedure, and, knowing the motives of his enemies, he remained unperturbed, coldly calm, maddeningly courteous, and serene, and he made his decisions instantly and perfectly. Time and again appeals were taken from his decisions, but he invariably was sustained. He never was confused, he never lost his temper, he never backed away from an embarrassing decision. It was at a time when the abolitionists were pouring petitions in upon the House, and John Quincy Adams, then a member, was forcing the issue. Himself unsympathetic toward abolitionist methods, and himself a slave-holder, he adhered rigidly to the right of petition. When Adams presented one of these petitions from a state other than his own, and protests were made against its reception, Polk ruled that "every member has a right to present a petition come from what quarter it may."

During Jackson's determined fight to force France to pay the spoliation claims from the Napoleonic period, the French were rattling the sword and threatening war, and the French fleet had sailed under sealed orders. Congress was on the verge of adjournment when Jackson asked the House to add $3,000,000 to the fortification bill for a possible emergency. When Polk used his influence to have the appropriation made, he was viciously attacked on the ground that he had not announced that the request had come from Jackson. At a critical moment, when war was threatened, a public announcement that Jackson was preparing for war would have added fuel to the fire.

After the passing of Jackson and the election of Martin Van Buren, Polk was reelected speaker of the House. The rowdyism of his enemies continued, reaching its rhetorical climax in his denunciation by the brilliant Mississippi orator, Seargent S. Prentiss, against whom Polk had decided in a contested election case. Prentiss was a master of vituperation and his purple patches were always memorable, but the purely personal inspiration of his attack stands out in his admission that he "did not deny the capacity of the Speaker, his despatch of business, or his full and thorough knowledge of parliamentary law." This speech was made when, at the close of Polk's second tenure, an unprecedented attempt was made by inflamed partisans to defeat the usual vote of thanks to the speaker. This was a significant tribute to the effectiveness of his leadership. No one doubted that he had presided with dignity and propriety. Just as Prentiss conceded his capacity and knowledge, the Boston *Age,* an organ of his enemies, in commenting on the indecent attacks on him, concluded that "it is but an act of justice to say of him that he discharged his duties with great ability, promptness, and throughout the session was popular with an immense majority of the members." In expressing his appreciation of the vote of thanks, Polk, with his usual good taste, ignored the petty action of his political enemies and thanked his friends; and men, who in response to the party whip had voted against the resolution, hastened to assure him of their personal regard. The opposition had been purely the emanation of partisan hate.

Here, then, was a man who for six epochal years of unequalled political controversy had led the party of Jefferson and Jackson in the House with such efficiency that he had incurred the hatred of political foes throughout the nation. Through these six dramatic years he had been among the foremost in the struggle. For four years he had presided over the greatest deliberative body of the nation with dignity and distinguished ability. His reputation was national.

For a brief period he was to pass from the national arena, but it was to serve a national purpose. The Jacksonians had lost Tennessee. This had resulted from the internal dissensions due to the feud between the followers of Jackson and the partisans of Senator White and John Bell. The loss of the state of Jackson was a humiliation to the old man in the Hermitage. The Jacksonians determined to wipe out the humiliation by redeeming Tennessee to the Democracy. Because of his high position nationally and his personal qualities, Polk was drafted to run for governor in 1839. To him it was a sacrifice. His interest was in national issues; his political associations were national in scope; and he enjoyed the work in Congress from which, in fourteen years, he had been absent but once because of illness. He made the sacrifice to restore the state to his party; and he made his campaign on national issues and was triumphant. But the rejoicing of the Jacksonians was premature. The party schism widened with the renomination of Van Buren in 1840, and in the elections of the next year the party went down in defeat in Tennessee. The next three years found Polk in retirement but in intimate touch with national politics. When President Tyler urged his acceptance of a place in the cabinet "without any pledge, shackle, or trammel being asked of you other than is already volunteered by your exalted character and standing," he declined the offer. Many had urged his nomination for Vice President with Van Buren in 1840.

IV

In the light of a record so distinguished in national politics it is remarkable that even a petty partisan of the sidewalks should have asked the question, "Who is Polk?" It is even more remarkable and discreditable that men presuming to write impartial history should have dignified the silly question by incorporating it in serious books, though for many years most historians were of the Federalist persuasion.

However, there is an explanation for the question propounded by the man in the street. The national career of Polk, however distinguished, had been confined to the House of Representatives at a time when popular interest was centered more upon the Senate with its galaxy of popular orators. It was at a time, a bit flamboyant in American history, when men of supreme eloquence appealed to the popular imagination. Polk made no pretense to eloquence, though as a logical and forceful debater he had few equals in his time. Again, these popular orators whose more picturesque passages were quoted in the streets and about the stoves in country stores, stood out familiarly in the minds of the multitude, and Polk's great arguments, cold, austere, logical, and closely knit, contained no such paragraphs. And again, these popular orators, traversing the country and addressing the excited crowds, were master showmen who dramatized their every action, and Polk had no gift for the dramatic and was incapable of showmanship.

Clay with his Olympian frown and captivating smile and Webster with his Jovian solemnity impressed the multitude, but there was nothing picturesque in the manner or appearance of Polk. Below the medium height, though commanding in his carriage, and, despite his finely molded head and broad brow, his manner at once urbane and decisive, and his impeccable attire, he could not attract special attention in a crowd. While the popular heroes appealed to the masses by sprinting gracefully from one purple patch to another, the mind of Polk was methodical, his reasoning logical, and his appeal in debate was to the mind and judgment, not to the emotions. There was nothing spectacular about him. The great orators of the time, with their sense of drama and skill in showmanship, could be popular on the television today, but Polk would have made only a limited appeal.

Again, Polk lacked magnetism, so essential to a popular leader, and unlike some of his contemporaries, he had no large personal following. He was essentially a serious thinker, and, aside from a few, he was prone to keep his thoughts to himself. He avoided unnecessary controversy when the public craved it. In his political correspondence he was so circumspect that a friend complained that though he had unburdened his mind to him he had found nothing in Polk's reply to illuminate his thinking: "I have not been able to even conjecture how your feelings are after all your long letters." This reticence did not draw casual acquaintances to him. His masterful control over his temper did not appeal to the masses who looked to their leaders for fighting words. To this day men quote the wit and humor of Clay and Lincoln, but Polk had little of that sense of humor that tickles the crowd. Take from Lincoln the voluminous illustrations of his humor, and much of his appeal to the average man would be lost. One would search far to find an illustration of Polk's humor. This was due in part to his incessant labor and his frail health that was failing under the pressure of his problems. Once some jugglers were performing at the White House to the immense amusement of everyone but Polk whose mind was remote from the scene. He records in his diary that during the exhibition his mind was on Oregon.

By nature he was formal, punctilious, cold, shy, and a bit sly, and people do not rally around these qualities with resounding cheers. He never lowered his dignity in pursuit of momentary popularity, and he never posed as Clay did constantly. If anything, he hid his light under a bushel. Though intimately identified with momentous decisions and the formulation of party and administrative policies under Jackson, he never claimed any credit. He never sought publicity for the part he played, and modesty is lost upon a crowd. The result was that, while the leaders knew his worth, the man in the street had no inkling of the importance of the part he played.

Here was a man of solid worth, without genius or the scintillation that goes with it, without personal magnetism, without a gift for self-dramatization, who reached conclusions through tireless research and who had few intimate friends. But long before anybody asked the question, "Who is Polk?", the Whigs were all too conscious of his ability. Horace Greeley had pronounced him "one of the ablest men and the most powerful speakers in the south west"; and Andrew Jackson, who knew men, had said that "his capacity for business [is] great—and to extraordinary powers of labor, both mental and physical, he unites that tact and judgment which are requisite to the successful direction of such an office as that of Chief Magistrate." And George Bancroft, the distinguished historian who worked beside him, has painted his portrait in a paragraph: "He was prudent, farsighted, bold, excelling any democrat of his time in undeviatingly correct exposition of democratic principles, and in short, as I think, judging of him as I know him by the results of his Administration, one of the foremost of our public men and one of the very best and most honest and most successful Presidents the country ever had."

That estimate is correct. The record proves that the nation owes an enormous debt of gratitude to Polk and to the brilliant success of his administration which in four short years solved grave problems that had baffled his predecessors; who brought a vast empire under the jurisdiction of the United States; who extended the national domain to the Pacific sea; who put a period to the bank controversy with his Constitutional Treasury; and whose enunciation of the Polk Doctrine definitively served notice on conspiring European monarchies that we would not tolerate the extension of their jurisdiction over a single inch of the North American continent.

V

That a man who did not aspire to the presidential nomination should have received it has puzzled some historians. It was without precedent, since the nomination went to a "dark horse" for the first time. It had been assumed that the nomination would go to Van Buren, and undoubtedly it would have, had he not made the irreparable blunder of taking a stand against the annexation of Texas. Without knowledge of Van Buren's letter, Polk, in reply to a note asking his position, had declared for "immediate annexation." Partly because of this and partly, as one has expressed it, because of Polk's "unterrified ability when leading the Jackson fight on the bank," some proposed to nominate Polk for Vice President to offset, in part, the unpopularity of Van Buren's position on Texas. Polk, convinced that defeat was certain unless the differences among the party leaders were smoothed out, set himself to the task, and one historian concludes that his suggestions "displayed that shrewdness and attention to detail which made him one of the most astute politicians of his time."

Meanwhile, Jackson, abandoning his favorite Van Buren because of his position on Texas, was writing Polk that he was the most available man because of his strong stand on Texas and because he came from the Southwest. Polk was astonished but not impressed. The Democratic convention balloted for three days with Van Buren far in the lead of Lewis Cass and others until the impossibility of his nomination was manifest. Meanwhile, delegates from Massachusetts, New York, and Pennsylvania agreed that the situation called for the nomination of Polk; the preference of Jackson had effect; and the supporters of Van Buren threw their votes to Polk, and he was nominated on the ninth ballot on the third day.

He entered the campaign with a unified party at his back. If the nomination amazed the little man in the street who did not know him, Henry Clay, who was nominated by the Whigs on a platform that ignored Texas and featured the tariff and the bank, was not amused. He was resting at his home at Ashland when his son rushed in and asked him to guess the winner. "Why Matty of course," said Clay. A negative nod from the son. "Then Cass." Another negative. "Then Buchanan." And still a nod in the negative. "Then who in the hell is he?" When told that his opponent would be Polk, an expression of annoyance passed over his face. "Beaten again, by God," he said; for Henry Clay, who had soft-pedaled on Texas with the assurance that Van Buren would be named, knew that the Democrats would have a popular issue and a unified party.

It was as Clay had foreseen. Polk received 170 electoral votes against 115, for Polk had carried New York, Pennsylvania, and New Hampshire on all of which Clay had pinned his hopes. And thus it came about that he who had not dreamed of the presidency began his journey to Washington. That his triumph brought him no delusions of grandeur is manifest in a letter to a friend asking him to secure quarters for him at the Coleman Hotel, "but," he added, "the rates must be reasonable and the bargain made in advance." He was inaugurated in the rain, or as John Quincy Adams wrote in his diary, in the presence of "a large assemblage of umbrellas." He had not yet reached his fiftieth year and no President before had attained the presidency so young.

His inaugural address left no doubt of his position on the three vital issues—he stood for the annexation of Texas, for the maintenance of our claims in Oregon, and for the reduction of the tariff to a revenue basis with such incidental protection as that basis might provide. And at the same time he took Bancroft into his confidence as to the program of his administration. He would annex Texas; he would try to acquire California; he would definitively settle the Oregon dispute with the English and maintain American rights; he would revise the tariff downward to a revenue basis that would be just to both the farmers and manufacturers; and he would put an end to the financial chaos and the bank controversy by the creation of a subtreasury, or as he preferred to call it a Constitutional Treasury. Meanwhile, he had pledged himself to one term. In four years he proposed to find a solution for problems that had been pending for years with no progress made. It was a herculean task he set himself.

VI

One item on the program, while vitally important at the time, proved to be of least permanent interest—the tariff. Throughout his life Polk had been a consistent opponent of protective tariffs. The platform on which he ran in 1844 contained no plank defining the party's position on this controversial subject, but he left no doubt of his position in his letter known as the Kane letter. Because of that letter some historians have said that he faced both ways, but the letter itself disproves the charge: "I am in favor of a tariff for revenue, such a one as will yield a sufficient amount to the Treasury to defray the expenses of the Government economically administered," and this would make possible a "reasonable incidental protection to our home industries." He clarified this in his second use of the word "protection" when he said that the tariff should be so framed as to give "fair and just protection to all the great interests of the whole Union, embracing agriculture, commerce and navigation."

This was not the protective tariff that Clay envisioned. His protection was for manufacturers alone, and in those days this was sectional. His plan made it possible for the manufacturer of the Northeast to sell in a protected market at artificial prices, while the farmer of the South and West would be forced, as before, to sell in the open market. Polk's position could not possibly have been misunderstood. In his address to the people when a candidate for governor, he had made his position crystal clear when he attacked the Clay concept of a protective tariff as one that "would take the property of one man and give it to another, without right or consideration," and would "depreciate the value of the productive industry of one section of the Union and transfer it to another," thus making the rich richer and the poor poorer.

The tariff, then dangerously sectional, had created an issue which had threatened to break the bonds that held the Union together; it had become the subject of acrimonious controversy leading to the nullification movement of Calhoun; and this had become so grave a threat to the Union that even Clay was compelled to come forward with his compromise tariff of 1833. This had provided for a biennial reduction until 1842, after which there was to be a uniform rate of twenty per cent; but in 1842 this was put aside for another protective tariff act which abandoned the revenue basis, and the nation again was threatened with a sectional issue. It was Polk's intention, if possible, to find a tariff formula based on the revenue basis which would be just to the nation as a whole and strike a fair balance between industry and agriculture.

In his inaugural address he had reiterated his tariff views, quoting from his Kane letter and saying that, in the framing of a tariff law, revenue should be the object and protection incidental. He made this clear: "In levying duties for revenue it is doubtless proper to make such discriminations within the revenue principle as will afford incidental protection to our home interests." This he followed in his first message with an expression of regret that nations did not consent to abolish all trade restrictions, but since this then was impossible, tariffs should be framed in a manner "calculated to avoid serious injury and to harmonize the conflicting interests of agriculture and manufactures." He had found that with a tariff fundamentally protective there was an accumulation of unnecessary revenue, and that the protected interests, instead of lowering the rates to make possible a lowering of cost to the consumer, found ways of getting rid of the money by reckless spending.

In his message he recommended immediate legislation "making suitable modifications and reductions" in the Tariff Act of 1842 which he described as primarily a protective measure. He insisted that rates should be kept within the revenue standard, and then he defined what he meant. He meant that when revenue diminished after a certain rate had been reached the rate should never go beyond. This was the limit of the revenue standard. And he challenged Clay by making tariff reform an administration measure.

This was a challenge to combat and drew the party line sharply. It made a major battle inevitable. Historians have ascribed the tariff bill to the pen of Robert J. Walker, Secretary of the Treasury, a brilliant Mississippian of sound judgment in economics and finance, because of his exhaustive report which accompanied the bill. It was a great document, but the bill itself was the work of Polk.

The struggle in Congress continued for weeks, and the little capital city swarmed with the lobbyists of the protected interests, abundantly provided for the entertainment of the lawmakers. The Whigs frothed, fumed, and tore passion to tatters with dire predictions of the disaster that would befall the country if the measure passed. Webster, in sepulchral tones, thought the bill "so novel, dangerous, so vicious in its general principles, so rash" that he foresaw a panic and depression with the victims starving in the streets. Polk wrote in his diary that the "monopolists have not surrendered the immense advantages which they possessed, and the enormous profits which they derived under the tariff of 1842, until after a fierce and mighty struggle. This city has swarmed with them for weeks." When the bill passed the House, Polk jubilantly recorded in his diary that it was "the most important domestic measure" of his administration.

The passage of the Walker tariff bill dealt a deadly blow at Clay's protective system, so deadly that it dared not raise its head again until years later during the War between the States; it gave such general satisfaction to the entire nation that for fifteen years and more no one found fault with its operation; it cleared the way for the administration's concentration on the vitally important international problems Polk had determined to solve; and instead of the tragic collapse of American economy so tearfully foreseen by Webster, the nation prospered under its operation. It has been recorded by history as one of the soundest tariff acts in the record of the republic.

Thus, Polk was able to draw his pen through one of the major achievements he had planned for his administration.

VII

Even in the midst of the struggle over the tariff, Polk was urgently pressing on Congress an Independent Treasury system that would definitively put a period to the confusion, amounting to chaos, that had continued from the beginning of Van Buren's administration. Jackson had destroyed the national bank of Biddle, and the dying money monopoly had sought its rehabilitation by an attempt to wreck the prosperity of the nation. On the removal of the government deposits from the bank they had been entrusted to state banks and this had not been satisfactory. Van Buren, the Jacksonians, and Polk were convinced that the government should collect its own money, through its own agents, and hold it in its own possession. The bitterness of the bank struggle had not abated. The minions of the old bank still clung to the hope that chaos and confusion would ultimately force the reestablishment of the institution conceived by Hamilton to serve the special interest of the moneyed class.

Throughout his administration Van Buren had brought all his not inconsiderable resources to bear on Congress for the creation of a subtreasury—a government institution holding the government's money, and that hard and not paper money. Still bent on the punishment of the nation for daring to destroy the national bank of Biddle, its minions in Congress fought the creation of a subtreasury tooth and nail; others who were hungering for plenty of paper money opposed it because the measure provided for the acceptance of hard money only. And Congress was in the possession of the enemy. Throughout his administration, Van Buren fought in vain. At length, toward the close he was able to get an Independent Treasury bill through Congress, but the first act of the next administration was to strike it down.

This was the dangerous situation as Polk entered the White House. Three years before he had come out for a subtreasury and hard money. He knew that both national and state banks had been unsatisfactory custodians of the nation's funds. He knew, or thought he knew, that it was not the idea of the framers of the Constitution that the nation's money should be entrusted to private corporations to use for private profit, and, at worst, for speculation. He did not believe that the money of the nation should have a direct connection with private banking institutions. He was convinced that the money of the people should be deposited in a treasury of the people, in possession of the people's agents directly responsible to the government whose money it was. Within seven weeks of his inauguration he was working on a bill for the creation of the nation's depository which he preferred to call the Constitutional Treasury. In his message, which the cabinet approved, he brushed aside the sophisticated reasoning of his opponents in a paragraph: "To say that the people or their Government are incompetent and not to be trusted with the custody of their own money in their own Treasury provided by themselves, but must rely on the presidents, cashiers, and stockholders of banking corporations, not appointed by them nor responsible to them, would be to concede that they are incapable of self-government."

One year after his inauguration his bill for the creation of a Constitutional Treasury that would receive metal money solely was presented to Congress and referred to the Committee on Ways and Means. The Whigs and the old minions of the defunct bank rallied to oppose it; the struggle was sharp, but the victory was won, and a building with fireproof vaults to be called the Treasury of the United States was under construction.

Thus, Polk succeeded where Van Buren had failed, and the controversy and confusion that had persisted from the day Jackson removed the deposits from the Bank of the United States and struck the fatal blow that ended its existence finally ended with the victory of Polk.

And so Polk was able to run his pen through another of the colossal tasks he had set for his administration.

VIII

When Polk took office, the problem of the northwestern boundary had been pending and unsolved for years. The question was whether the United States or England had a good title to all the territory west of the Rocky Mountains between the northern boundary of California and the southern boundary of Alaska. The British based their claim on explorations made by Captain James Cook in 1778; they laid claim to the interior of the Oregon region because of the discovery of the Fraser River and its valley by Alexander Mackenzie in 1793. To all this region the Spaniards had laid claim, and a war between Spain and England was barely averted by their treaty of 1790 which granted trading posts to the British; but it was not made clear whether this meant British ownership of the land or merely its momentary use.

The United States laid claim to the region partly on concession from Spain and France and partly on the discoveries and settlements of the Americans. In 1792 Captain Robert Gray of Boston had explored the Columbia River and had named it after his ship, and in 1811 John Jacob Astor had established a trading post at Astoria.

During the administration of Monroe an Anglo-American treaty fixed the boundary at the forty-ninth parallel from the Great Lakes to the Rockies, and all the country west of the Rockies was left open for the joint occupation of the nationals of both nations. This merely meant that the nationals of each could occupy it without prejudice to either. In 1827 this agreement was indefinitely extended, but with the provision that it could be terminated on a year's notice by either the United States or England. When, four years later, the English extended their laws over this territory, there was trouble in the offing. During the administration of John Quincy Adams a bill was introduced in Congress to extend the laws of the United States over the same territory and to build forts for the protection of the Americans. It is significant that Polk opposed this measure on the ground that it violated the treaty of joint occupation, and that this treaty, right or wrong, was the law of the land until its abrogation on a year's notice.

In 1842 during the administration of John Tyler a resolution was passed by the Senate providing for the construction of forts along the route to Oregon and for the granting of land to American settlers. The House had adjourned without taking action on this resolution, but the congressional debate that ensued brought the Oregon question to the forefront. Strong language was used, and the press was not more moderate in its tone. The threatening attitude of the British dramatized the situation; Palmerston, the sword-rattling foreign minister of England, declared that the passage of the resolution would mean war. The Tyler administration accomplished nothing, and thus the Oregon question entered conspicuously into the presidential campaign of 1844.

The Democratic platform that year laid claim to the whole of Oregon, and the extremists of the Northwest became vociferous in their demand for the entire territory extending beyond the forty-ninth parallel into what is now Canada, and their slogan of "Fifty-four forty or fight!" resounded with a roar. This inevitably would put the Democratic nominee, if triumphant, in an embarrassing position. If he backed away from the extreme demand, he would be charged with repudiating the platform; if he was prepared to fight for the whole, he faced the possibility of war with England.

In his inaugural address Polk declared that "our title to the country of the Oregon is clear and unquestionable," and though he did not say all of the country, this was assumed. The reaction in England was one of incredulity. Lord Aberdeen sought to soften the blow by promising a peaceful settlement through negotiations, but even so, he declared the English claims just, and he promised that they would be maintained. The London *Times,* spouting fury, threatened war. Far off at the Hermitage the dying Jackson raged over the British threat. He wrote Polk that the British claims should be rejected bluntly: "This is the rattling of British drums to alarm us."

Polk, more circumspect, decided to renew the offer of Tyler, to which he felt himself committed, to compromise on the forty-ninth parallel, and he sent Louis McLane, an able diplomat, to London as minister. Replying then to the British note which had asked us to suggest an equitable settlement, Secretary of State James Buchanan, on instructions from Polk, offered the forty-ninth parallel as the northern boundary. In explaining his action to McLane, Polk said that he was "called upon to decide whether to break off or continue negotiations." Placed in a position of high responsibility he had asked himself whether the national honor demanded that he abruptly terminate negotiations, or lay claim to the whole of the territory extending to the southern boundary of Alaska. He found himself embarrassed, if not committed, by Tyler's offer of the forty-ninth parallel. He instructed Buchanan to propose that the Oregon country be divided at the forty-ninth parallel from the Rocky Mountains to the Pacific, with free ports for the British on that part of Vancouver Island lying south of that parallel.

When Richard Pakenham, the British minister, insolently rejected the offer, Polk, in indignation, withdrew the offer and laid claim to the whole of the territory, personally dictating the reply. He instructed Buchanan to "assert and enforce our right to the whole of the Oregon territory" and to say that he had offered the forty-ninth parallel in deference to his predecessor and his desire for peace. But since Pakenham had rejected the offer without even submitting it to his government in London, it was now withdrawn. With the super-caution that characterized him, Buchanan proposed that the reply should say that any proposition coming from Pakenham would be considered, but Polk refused: "Let our proposition be absolutely withdrawn & then let the British Minister take his own course." Buchanan begged to delay sending the reply. Polk ordered its immediate transmission. The reply was a strong state document and was all the stronger because the rejected offer had received such scurvy treatment from the British minister. Polk had learned that the British government was eager for a settlement and that the principal obstacle was the opposition of the British Hudson's Bay Company.

Some weeks intervened with nothing more done, but Polk had learned that Lord Aberdeen, regretting that Pakenham had not submitted the offer of the forty-ninth degree, had expressed the hope that we would reopen negotiations. Assuming that Pakenham had received instructions to this effect, Buchanan asked Polk what answer should be given. He was told that if the British had any proposition to make it would be received and considered, but that no intimation should be given as to our views or intentions. If the minister proposed to agree to the previous offer of compromise it should be rejected; if any other proposition was made, Polk would refer it to the Senate for advice.

He told the cabinet, however, that in his message he would "maintain all our rights and would reaffirm Mr. Monroe's position against permitting any European power to establish any colony on the North American continent." In conference with Benton it was agreed that the twelve months' notice for the abrogation of the convention of 1827 should be given, that the laws of the United States should be spread over Oregon to the same degree as British laws had been extended in 1831, and that forts should be built en route to Oregon. Benton favored the forty-ninth parallel in the belief that the British had claims north of that point.

Meanwhile, Pakenham's note arrived, and with his usual ineptitude he said the note could be treated as official or unofficial as we thought fit. Under this stipulation it was refused and the note withdrawn.

It was then that Polk sat down to the preparation of his message to Congress. Buchanan urged that he soft-pedal his position, and Polk refused. It was at this time that his relations with Buchanan were strained. Unquestionably he seriously doubted the loyalty of his Secretary of State, and as a protection to himself he began keeping the diary which has been such a rich mine of information to the historians. There he wrote that "Mr Buchanan has been from the beginning too timid and too fearful of war, and has been most anxious to settle the question by yielding and making more concessions than I am willing to make." Polk had no fear that England would go to war. He knew that there was much distress in England and protest over the corn laws; that England's relations with France were strained to the breaking point; and that because of the famine in Ireland the people were seething there. With this knowledge he wrote his message in uncompromising terms, and he recommended that notice should be given of the abrogation of the agreement of 1827. He would force the issue.

Thoroughly convinced now that Polk was in deadly earnest, Pakenham proposed arbitration by some sovereign state or European monarch. The proposal was instantly rejected on the ground that acceptance of arbitration would be an assumption that Great Britain's title was as good as America's.

Meanwhile, the military and naval committees of the House were instructed to inquire into the defensive needs of the country. Polk had said that "it is better to fight for the first inch of national territory than for the last." Congress responded with the notice of the abrogation of the settlement of 1827, and with plans for the organization of a government in Oregon. And, for the first time through the administrations of Monroe, Adams, Jackson, Van Buren, and Tyler, England knew that she could no longer procrastinate or bluff.

Polk had maintained his claim to the entire territory because he felt bound by his party's platform, but in his own mind he shared Benton's doubts as to our rights to the whole of it. Word was conveyed to Aberdeen that should the British propose the forty-ninth parallel it would be favorably received, and Aberdeen, eager to avoid war, was quick to respond. He made the proposal with the reservation that the British settlers and the Hudson's Bay Company should retain title to the lands they held south of the forty-ninth parallel, but retain them subject to the laws of the United States. Polk submitted the proposal to the Senate for advice, and by a vote of thirty-seven to twelve the Senate advised acceptance.

Thus, after many years of controversy, Polk had forced the issue. By insisting on the abrogation of the settlement of 1827 he brought the issue to a head. By his stanch stand he had shaken the complacency of London which had retained its supercilious attitude toward the young republic. And the settlement of the boundary between the United States and Canada had been just and fair and had left no grievances with our good friends across the northern frontier. He had been right in his theory that at that time the way to deal with John Bull "was to look him straight in the eye." By his action he had forced the recognition of undoubted American territorial rights, and by his triumph the great states of Oregon, Washington, Idaho, and parts of Montana and Wyoming came concededly under the jurisdiction of the United States, and the American flag was firmly planted on the Pacific.

And so Polk drew his pen through another of the incredible tasks he had set for his administration.

IX

Polk had now succeeded where others had failed in carrying out three of the difficult purposes he had set his administration, but his eyes were fixed on Texas, and beyond Texas on New Mexico and California.

The people of Texas had declared their independence of Mexico in the spirit of 1836, but the Jackson administration wisely had held back on recognition until the formation of a government and the adoption of a constitution. It had listened, sympathetically, no doubt, but in silence to the Texans' plea for annexation. Meanwhile, Texas had a government and a leader of power and popularity in the picturesque Sam Houston. In the year of Polk's election, Houston, then retiring from the presidency of Texas, not only had concluded that annexation to the United States—so long frowned upon—would not be an unmixed blessing, but shockingly appears to have been willing to form an alliance with England and France on the basis of Texan independence.

The administration of Tyler was keen for annexation. Only a few days before the inauguration of Polk, Congress had authorized the annexation of Texas whenever the government of Texas asked it and conformed to certain conditions; and one day before Polk's inauguration, Tyler had sent Andrew Jackson Donelson, as our chargé d'affaires, to work out the details in accordance with the annexation resolution of the House. Polk instructed the chargé to take no action pending instructions from the new administration. Buchanan, the new Secretary of State, had not yet arrived in Washington.

Meanwhile, Polk was in possession of disturbing reports from the American minister in London of the active efforts of England and France to dissuade the Texans from annexation to the United States. The British envoy had promised to secure the recognition of the Republic of Texas, and, in addition, to give it a profitable commercial agreement. His conduct was openly hostile and violated all international usage. At the same time Houston was holding back on annexation until he visited Jackson at the Hermitage; soon Jackson wrote jubilantly that the Black Raven had now "put his shoulder to the wheel," and that Texas could not be bought with British gold. With sentiment overwhelmingly in favor of annexation, the British envoy tried another tack. He warned that annexation would be followed by a declaration of war by Mexico; that this would lead to an American blockade of Mexican ports; that this would not be tolerated by England, and that a war would follow that would continue for twenty years. As we shall see, nothing could so arouse the fighting blood of Polk as interference by a European power on the American continent.

While the English, possibly with the French in conjunction, were exerting themselves by means not recognized in international affairs to prevent the annexation, the Mexican minister in Washington was protesting against it and threatening war in the event of its consummation. He demanded his passports. He was informed that it was too late to discuss the independence of Texas, and that since the independent Texans had petitioned for annexation this had now become the will of the United States.

With Mexico openly threatening war on Texas to recover its possessions, the Texas republic was in fear of an invasion on a large scale. Polk gave assurance that the moment Texas was annexed by the will of its people expressed in its congress and voted by the people, he would "then conceive it to be both his right and his duty" to defend "that State against the attacks of any foreign power." He announced that 3,000 soldiers would be placed immediately on the Texas border to enter the state on a moment's notice. He had been reliably informed that Mexico was concentrating troops on the Rio Grande, where Texas had no army posts, and would invade to the Nueces River. Polk was asked what we would do should an invasion take place before the Texas congress had formally accepted annexation. He replied that protection would be given after American annexation had been voted by the Texas congress, but he personally gave assurance that in view of an invading Mexican army and the open interference of the British, he was "resolved to defend and protect Texas, as far as I possess the power to do so." He had ordered our troops to march at once to the mouth of the Sabine River, and he had ordered a naval force to the Gulf of Mexico. But he made it clear that immediate action by the Texas congress was imperative. Once it had taken action, he said, "I shall regard Texas as part of the Union; all questions of Constitutional power to defend & protect her by driving an invading Mexican Army out of her Territory will be at an end and our land and naval forces will be under orders to do so."

The Texas congress was promptly convened. The conditional recognition of Texas independence offered by the British was rejected, and unanimously the congress voted for annexation, adopted a constitution, and submitted both the constitution and the resolution of annexation to the people who approved both by an overwhelming majority. The Lone Star State was now a part of the Union.

This is the point where Polk was challenged by the Whigs as to the propriety of his action. In the American resolution of annexation there had been no clear definition of the boundaries of Texas. Under an agreement with Mexico in 1836 the Texans laid claim to all the territory up to the Rio Grande by right of the Louisiana Purchase. The Mexicans not only repudiated this agreement; they now laid claim to the whole of Texas. They had a few army posts in the disputed territory; the Texans had none. Polk had instructed his emissary that the boundary settlement was to be reached through negotiations and that he hoped to avoid a war. But he had learned that Mexico was preparing an invasion of this territory in force with a view to the ultimate recovery of the whole of Texas now a part of the United States. He therefore ordered United States troops up to the Rio Grande. The military posts of the Mexicans were not to be molested pending negotiations. If, however, an attack was made, it was to be repelled, and the Mexican army east of the Rio Grande was to be expelled. He did not believe that Mexico wanted war. The movement of troops was in the nature of a warning. Texas, now part of the Union, laid claim to the country east of the Rio Grande, and Polk supported their contention. It may be conceded that by the assertion of this claim he may have gone a little far, but he had offered and urged negotiations, and they had been refused.

Meanwhile, he had been informed by his emissary in the City of Mexico that the Mexicans were willing to negotiate the differences as to this disputed strip if he would send a commissioner. Acting instantly on this information, Polk sent John Slidell, a competent man, as minister, and Mexico refused to receive him on the ground that he was a minister and not a commissioner. Slidell had gone with reasonable instructions. He was to negotiate. If possible, he was to purchase New Mexico and California, and he was authorized to go as high as $40,000,000. Polk was increasingly concerned over the activities of the British agent in California. Here was an opportunity to effect a complete settlement of the various problems without war.

But Slidell, on reaching the Mexican capital, was confronted by childish haggling. The president refused to receive him; and when that executive went out and another came in who likewise refused to receive him, it was clear that Mexico had no thought of negotiations. Polk wrote that if the refusal continued, "the cup of forbearance will then have been exhausted"; that the failure to receive the minister would be an insult to the United States. He instructed Slidell that "every honorable effort should be made before a final rupture," but, unless soon received, he should demand his passports and Polk would submit the facts to the American Congress. He was not received, and he demanded his passports. Before returning to Washington to report he was told that Mexico considered not the occupation of disputed territory, but the annexation of Texas as a cause of war.

Meanwhile, sixteen American dragoons were killed by

Mexican armed forces. Polk prepared his message to Congress, and the war was on.

The Whigs and abolitionists were to contend that the sending of troops into the disputed territory was wrong and that Polk had forced war on Mexico; they ignored the fact that Mexico used this as an excuse for war which they began for the recovery of Texas which was now a state of the American Union.

It is significant that Buchanan proposed that the declaration of war should say that the United States had no thought of acquiring California or New Mexico. Polk refused. He was determined if possible to acquire both, preferably through purchase. When Buchanan warned that Lord Aberdeen would demand to know whether we had any thought of California and would threaten, in such an event, a war against us by both England and France, Polk hotly replied that "before I would make the pledge which he proposed, I would meet the war which either England or France or all the Powers of Christendom might wage" and that "neither as a citizen nor as President would I permit or tolerate any intermeddling of any European Power on this Continent." He announced his determination, if possible, "honorably and fairly of acquiring California." There is every reason to believe that when war with Mexico began, the mind of Polk was centered on California.

The waging of the war and the gallantry and resourcefulness of our soldiers has been luminously written into the history of American valor. Ignoring party politics, Polk gave the supreme command to two Whig generals. Neither was loyal to him, Winfield Scott because of his fantastic vanity and Zachary Taylor because of a totally unjustified suspicion that Polk did not appreciate his services. Then, too, Taylor was not interested in California.

Even in the midst of the war Polk hoped for a termination

through negotiations, and he even had envoys with the armies ready at any moment to end the conflict. But events moved rapidly. When in August, 1846, Colonel Philip Kearny made his heroic march overland to Santa Fe and took possession without a battle, New Mexico fell to the United States. Thus was realized one of Polk's aspirations, and thus he found a base for military operations against California.

He was motivated in his desire for California by two reasons. One was his ardent desire for the Pacific coast from Mexico to Canada; the other was his conviction that the British especially, and the French to a lesser degree, were bent on the planting of colonies in California. This was intolerable to Polk. He hoped to bring that great state under American jurisdiction without strife with the people living there. He had instructed American agents there that if California followed in the wake of Texas and preferred its independence, the United States would be its friend; but should she, like Texas, wish an affiliation with this country, she would be warmly welcomed. However, no encouragement should be given to attempt a conquest. He wished California to come into the Union as a friend and not be dragged in regardless of her wishes. Even so he was prepared to take advantage of any opportunity the war might offer. He ordered that an expeditionary force be prepared against northern California and be on the ground when the war closed. He had given instructions that when war came the navy should take possession of the great port of San Francisco. In all this he again differed from Buchanan who was against holding California north of Monterey. The sword-rattling adventure of John C. Frémont was on his own responsibility and against the policy of Polk, though Polk never for a moment took his eyes off California.

When the war ended with victory, America was in possession of the country up to the Rio Grande, as Polk had planned; New Mexico had virtually been won when Santa Fe surrendered without a fight; and Polk was in a position to take California as one of the fruits of triumph and without compensation to Mexico.

It is certainly true that England was seeking in every way to prevent American acquisition of California; certain it is that Aberdeen had instructed his agent in Mexico that, should California break away from Mexico, England would view with extreme displeasure the establishment of a protectorate over her by any other nation. Unquestionably Aberdeen had discussed with the Mexican diplomat in London a plan for colonization in California which would furnish his government with an excuse for intervention; and he had discussed with this diplomat a scheme for mortgaging Mexican lands in California to an English company. And the Mexican minister had informed his government that, if France would go along, England was ready for a war on that issue with the United States.

Polk was equally determined on his policy. Any attempt by England or any other power would be resisted by the United States. Polk instructed his envoy that in the negotiation of the peace treaty he was to claim the disputed boundary of Texas up to the Rio Grande and to insist on the ceding of California and New Mexico. Mexico was paid in return for the ceding $15,000,000—less than half what Polk had been prepared to pay but a short time before.

And so, with the ratification of the Treaty of Guadalupe Hidalgo, California, New Mexico, Arizona, Nevada, Utah, and some of Colorado became parts of the United States, and America faced immediately on the Pacific sea from Mexico to Canada, and one of the most difficult of the tasks Polk had set for his administration was completed.

Who is Polk? Why he is the man who brought more

vitally important territory under the jurisdiction of the Stars and Stripes than had been brought since Jefferson's purchase of Louisiana, or has ever been brought in the more than a century that has intervened.

Polk had solved the disturbing currency problem pending for ten years by the establishment of the Independent Treasury. He had revised the tariff with an act so fitted to conditions that no one proposed its alteration for more than sixteen years. He had solved the problem of Oregon after many years of unsuccessful efforts and thus had given Oregon, Washington, Idaho, and parts of Montana and Wyoming to the United States. He had made the definitive answer to the question of Texas, had extended its boundary to the Rio Grande, had acquired New Mexico and Arizona, and had brought California under the flag just when gold was discovered and the gold rush began.

The realization of the incredibly difficult program he had outlined for an administration of four years was due to Polk's vision, his courage, his diplomacy and statesmanship, and his stern determination and indifference to abuse in the service of the republic.

X

And out of all this emerges what has been called the Polk Doctrine which was something new in our international policy and which has been followed from that day to this. Polk had abundant evidence of an offensive meddling of European powers in the affairs of the American continent. England and France had interfered with cynical contempt for international usage in Texas. They had interfered similarly in California. In the French chamber of deputies one speaker had let the cat out of the bag with the statement that France was pledged to support England in a war to prevent the annexation of Texas.

Premier Guizot was forced to cover a retreat with the statement that, while Texas could do as it wished, there were higher considerations. And what were these? He made it plain that France was eager to impose on America the balance of power system in vogue in Europe. His meaning was transparent. England, Spain, and the United States had possessions in the New World, and he meant the creation of a system that could prevent American predominance on this continent. It was common knowledge, too, that some European nations were planning to establish a monarchy in Mexico under a European king, currently reported to be the Spanish Prince Henry.

Confronted by these undoubted threats, Polk met them in a message to Congress which was more historical than many historians seem to realize. Referring to the efforts of European monarchies to interfere in American affairs, he warned that American sentiment would not tolerate it. Apropos of Guizot's amazing confession as to the balance of power, he declared that its purpose was to prevent American advance. Then Polk laid down the law: "The United States, sincerely desirous of preserving relations of good understanding with all nations, can not in silence permit any European interference on the North American continent, and should any such interference be attempted, will be ready to resist it at any and all hazards." And then he added that it was proper to reaffirm the principles avowed by Monroe and to announce "to the world as our settled policy that no future European colony or dominion shall with our consent be planted or established on any part of the North American continent."

This went beyond the Monroe Doctrine with the declaration that we would not tolerate the sale or transfer, even with the consent of the people, of any section of the continent. He made it clear that the "existing rights" of nations already in possession would be respected. The London *Times* preferred to ignore the words "existing rights" to pounce indignantly on Polk as having threatened such British possessions as Canada.

Not only did he announce a new doctrine, but he acted in accordance. At a time when the Hawaiian Islands were attracting the attention of the English for commercial reasons, Polk sent instructions to our agent there that it was important for the islands to remain an independent nation and to make known that "we could not view with indifference their transfer to, or dependence upon any European Power."

And Cuba? He would have purchased the island had it been for sale. He would not have it on any other condition. He made an offer to Spain of $100,000,000 which was refused. He frowned upon American connivance in any subversive movement there. But when Lord George Bentinck, referring to Cuba's heavy debt to Britain, suggested that England had the power to go to war and collect the money by taking over the revenue, the Polk Doctrine was a sufficient warning.

The doctrine was for the protection of the United States. It was not imperialist, since Polk was not. When Buchanan proposed during the Mexican trouble that we take the whole region west of the Sierra Madre Mountains, and Walker urged the taking of the whole of Mexico, Polk rebuked them by a stern refusal to consider such action. When the king of Sweden offered the island of Saint Barthélemy, Polk politely refused it with the explanation that "the acquisition of distant insular possessions for colonial dependencies has never been deemed desirable by the United States."

The Whigs and the political enemies of Polk have been critical, however, of his words and actions in the case of Yucatan. What was it all about? During the Mexican War, Yucatan remained neutral, and to that extent America was obligated to her. Because of her neutrality she lost the protection of the Mexican government and army. Taking advantage of this situation, the Indians, enormously outnumbering the whites, were threatening their extermination. A commissioner from Yucatan appeared in Washington asking for military assistance as a protection against extermination. At first reluctant, Polk finally authorized Commodore Matthew C. Perry to supply the whites with ammunition if certain that it would not be used outside Yucatan. To make the problem graver the governor of the province, in a formal communication on the threatened extermination of the whites, said that his people were "ready to surrender their country & the sovereignty over it to any Government which would protect & save them from extermination." What gravely disturbed Polk was the admission that a similar offer had been made to England and Spain.

Here was a direct challenge to the Polk Doctrine. He did not want one inch of Yucatan, but he did not want one inch to go to a European power. He told his cabinet that "we could never agree to see Yucatan pass into the hands of a foreign monarchy, to be possessed and colonized by them, and that sooner than this should take place the United States would afford the aid and protection asked," but he added that this could be done only through an act of Congress. He prepared the rough draft of his intended message and read it to his cabinet which approved. He set forth the offer to the United States and also to Spain and England. He made clear that he had no intention or desire to take over the dominion and sovereignty of that province, but that we could not, and would not, permit England or Spain to do so. His one recommendation to Congress was to "adopt such measures as in their judgment may be expedient to prevent Yucatan from becoming a colony of any European power." A resolution was introduced authorizing the President "to take temporary military occupation of Yucatan." However, nothing of the sort was necessary or done, since, in the meanwhile, the government of Yucatan had reached a satisfactory agreement with the Indians, and the danger of extermination of the whites was over.

The only possible ground for criticism here has been based on what is known not to be true—that Polk was planning to take over the sovereignty of the country against which he had officially pledged himself.

From the hour Polk enunciated his doctrine it has been the doctrine of the United States, and it takes its place with the Monroe Doctrine on which it was an advance. Years later, after Polk was sleeping in the garden of Polk Place, the European powers, taking advantage of American preoccupation with the War between the States, set up a monarchy in Mexico and placed the ill-fated Maximilian of Austria upon the throne. The moment our war was over, his fate was sealed. The monarchs knew that the gallant men who had worn the blue and the men who had worn the gray, all Americans and all patriots, would have closed ranks and marched as one to the expulsion of the European pretender to the throne of Mexico. The knees of Napoleon the Little began to wobble; he withdrew his armed men; he betrayed Maximilian's trust in him. The monarch of Mexico died miserably before a firing squad, and the unhappy Carlotta lingered through many years a mental wreck, living in a world of fantasies and dreams. But the Polk Doctrine remains, and no European nation would dare today to attempt its violation.

XI

Never robust, this tense, continuous concentration on his work drew heavily upon Polk's vitality. Accustomed to horseback riding for exercise, he wrote in his diary that his fine saddle horse had not been out of the stable for months. He lacked the gift of putting a period to his labors for relaxation. His mind was highly geared. Even in the midst of social functions his thoughts were remote from the scene, and, if the social life in the White House was delightful, this was due to the great charm and cleverness of his accomplished wife to whom even his worst enemies paid tribute. His mind was of the sort that can never rest. He insisted that all negotiations of an international character, and there were many, should be conducted in Washington under his direct supervision. Not least among his annoyances were those that came from the presidential aspirations of Buchanan, his Secretary of State. Buchanan was an able man, an accomplished diplomat, a clever politician, but Polk found him a bit slippery in that he sometimes shifted his position to meet the breeze of momentary public opinion. Buchanan was supercautious. He lacked both the courage and the daring of his chief. The record shows that he differed frequently with the President on vital issues and that in every instance it was the President that prevailed. The important decisions were Polk's alone. He dictated the tone and substance of Buchanan's diplomatic notes, but, forced to follow instructions, Buchanan could be counted on to make them impressively strong. The truth is that Polk was his own cabinet. He did not ask the members for written reports, preferring that these be made in full council where they could be known and discussed. Once, after observing the twisting of Buchanan, he wrote in his diary that no candidate for President should be given a post in the cabinet.

He had lofty ideals of the proprieties. Once an admirer presented him with a valuable horse, and it was returned with a note of thanks. When another admirer sent him some choice wines and table delicacies, he demanded the bill that he might pay. His honesty was proverbial.

Though he often differed sharply with friends on public issues and old ties were momentarily broken, he did not make a fetish of his resentments. He broke with Benton, and it was easy to break with that dictatorial statesman, but a reconciliation was effected and the old relations renewed. When Senator Hannegan, a brilliant man gifted with superb eloquence, attacked him in a bitter philippic, and soon thereafter lost his seat in the Senate, Polk made him our first minister to Prussia. He did not cultivate hates.

Under the tremendous pressure, working toward the achievement of the almost incredible program he had outlined for his administration, his health—never good—suffered, and his physical strength diminished, but he refused to rest. Toward the end of his administration, he was convinced that death was not remote. He wrote in his diary, "I am heartily rejoiced that my term is so near its close."

His conduct at the inauguration of his successor was courtly and impeccably proper. General Taylor had been made by him. It was his triumphs as a soldier that the people acclaimed, and it was Polk who had made these triumphs possible. Though Taylor was far from loyal to his chief, he was not molested in his command. Polk gave him a dinner after his successor had called at the White House, and he rode with him to the Capitol. And then Polk turned longingly to his home in Tennessee. His journey home drew heavily on his strength. At Richmond, at Charleston, at New Orleans, and on the journey up the Mississippi he was acclaimed at notable receptions. He was on the verge of collapse when he reached Nashville.

There he had bought the old home of his friend and mentor, Felix Grundy, and called it Polk Place. Was there a touch of sentiment in the acquisition of the home of the statesman and orator who had been his friend in the early days? I like to think there was. There he busied himself with the arrangement of his books and papers and in puttering about his garden in the distribution of his flowers, but even this drew heavily on his strength. There he passed soon to his accounting at the early age of fifty-four and was buried on the grounds. Later, the people of the state he had so singularly honored gave him and his lovely wife a grave and monument on the grounds of the State House.

Four years only in the loftiest station in the world, and what had he achieved? His tariff policy led to prosperity and some semblance of sectional peace for fifteen years. His Constitutional Treasury idea proved to be sound. His single administration gave this country the Pacific coast from Mexico to Canada. His Polk Doctrine served notice on Europe that the United States never would tolerate interference on this continent and never would permit the balance of power plan of Guizot and the Old World to check the advance of its people in North America.

Few Presidents can duplicate his record. Jefferson alone has stamped his name on so much of American geography.

The political party that hated him has been dead and buried for a century; the issue used against him by the fanaticism of the abolitionists died almost a century ago with the Emancipation Proclamation; but the vast empire he gave the republic is here to proclaim his right to the gratitude of the nation. I hope the time will come when a statue of heroic proportions will be raised in San Francisco facing the Golden Gate, from which he never took his eyes until that beautiful city and great port unfurled the American flag to the breezes of the Pacific sea.

3

ANDREW JACKSON

His Substitution of Party Government for Personal Politics

I

THE REIGN of Andrew Jackson ushered in a new day in American political life. It organized the methods of a functional democracy. He had been swept into office despite the opposition of a major part of the press, the moneyed element, and the political leaders of long-established reputation. His support came from the mass of the people. Many of these were newly enfranchised, and his problem was to organize and consolidate this mass into a compact party capable of encountering the bitter opposition of the Clays, the Websters, and the Calhouns.

This called for political genius of a high order, and he surrounded himself with a small group of practical politicians known to history a bit contemptuously as the Kitchen Cabinet. He found the nation drifting toward personal government tending to the confusion of the people as to policies and principles. It was because he himself was a masterful politician that he surrounded himself with politicians with technique, although some historians of the Federalist persuasion have tried to belittle him and to dismiss his political entourage as composed of men of small minds. These gentlemen of the academy who make a pose of their distaste for politics unwittingly expose themselves as poor material for a democracy. Since politics is the science, and sometimes the art, of government, he who is too precious to soil his mind with politics deserves the bad government that would be inevitable if a majority of the people were equally precious.

In politics there must be politicians trained in the science and art of managing men and directing public opinion; and, in a democracy such as ours, there must be political parties to clearly formulate policies and support principles on which the people may intelligently pass, or we would have a chaotic society.

If England has been intelligently ruled for 200 years it is because there have been two major parties with opposing views between which the people have been able to determine at the polls. The party in power has the responsibility; the function of the party out of power is equally important in its role of critic. That is the reason that it is known in England as His Majesty's Opposition. If the people are dissatisfied with their government, the party of the opposition, similarly dissatisfied, presents definite alternatives to the policies of those in power, and the people can determine intelligently what they want to do.

At the present time when political parties and politicians seem to be anathema to idealistic theorists, the political scientists of the drawing room and the library, it is not without significance that they are equally obnoxious to the totalitarians, both of the right and left. Many editorial writers, columnists, and radio commentators exhaust their vocabulary of contempt on party government and politicians. These condescend to ascribe statesmanship to their favored few, without observing that even their favorites were the most successful politicians of their generation. These supercilious gentlemen of the cloister and the swivel chair find it convenient to ignore the fact that these gifted politicians would never have found an opportunity to prove their statesmanship had they not reached their commanding station in the hurly-burly of party politics.

In England from the days of Sir Robert Walpole down through Pitt, Fox, Palmerston, Gladstone and Disraeli, Lloyd George and Churchill, the great statesmen have invariably been the great politicians; and in our country they who disdain the politician wear blinders to the fact that the greatest of our statesmen from Jefferson down through Jackson, Lincoln, and Franklin Roosevelt have been the most consummate politicians of their generation.

And so for a full generation the politician has been the target of derision from gentlemen with theories who have not the slightest conception of the art of directing and governing men. Long ago Montaigne, in one of his essays, observed that no one has a good opinion of a politician. Before Montaigne, Sir Walter Raleigh, no mean politician himself but unhappily for him then out of favor, wrote some doggerel:

Tall men of high condition
That manage the Estate,
Their purpose is ambition.
Their practice only hate.
And if they once reply
Then give them all the lie.

The brilliant Scotch historian and philosopher, F. S. Oliver, in his fascinating and colorful study of Walpole's time, *The Endless Adventure,* takes sharp issue with the baiters of politicians though he himself was primarily an intellectual of the closet:

Even ordinary people like ourselves find it impossible to rid our minds of the delusion that "in essentials" we are better men than these noisy, lime-seeking busy-

> bodies. And as we read our newspapers we are encouraged in the comfortable belief that our moral and intellectual superiority, though we wear it modestly, is never for a moment in danger of being overlooked by Almighty God. What a humbug it is for the most part. And what a welter we would be in if the politicians, taking our lectures to heart, were to hand over the management of public affairs to their critics.

His point is that without organized parties, based on principles and policies, and submitting these to the arbitrament of the people at the polls, the functioning of democracy would be impossible; and without political parties sponsoring specific policies and principles, purely personal politics, inspired solely by personal ambitions, would bring a babble of jarring voices full of sound and fury signifying nothing but the utter confusion of the people.

II

From 1809, the closing year of the Jefferson regime, American Presidents were chosen by the caucus system in which the people had a minor part. The group with a majority in Congress met in caucus and designated the candidate. At the beginning of the second Monroe administration the old Federalist party, thoroughly discredited, had ceased to exist as a national organization, and the only political party was the Republican party of Jefferson. Into this party the remaining Federalists had pretended to merge on the theory that if you cannot lick the enemy you should join him. This state of affairs brought in what is ironically called the "era of good feeling," but among the ambitious aspiring to power, the symbol of this misnamed era was the battle-ax and the stiletto.

This was a perilous period—this era of good feeling—since with no definite and avowed opposing political principles and policies embodied in a political party, we were rushing toward a government, not of principles or policies, but of individuals, with the issues submerged beneath the vision of the people.

With only one avowed party, in the cabinet of Monroe were three men of impressive stature, each panting for the presidency. There was John Quincy Adams, honest, able, but self-centered and quarrelsome, Secretary of State; there was John C. Calhoun, a great statesman and political scientist, one of the greatest of Americans, Secretary of War; and there was William H. Crawford, a resourceful politician with a distinguished record of public service. All these men were pursuing the presidency with a morbid intensity, and naturally they did not dwell together in harmony. Outside the cabinet was Henry Clay who sought, and for twenty years was to intrigue, for the presidency; and outside the caucus group was Andrew Jackson, the favorite of the people, who, until then, had been given scant consideration in the arena of national politics.

All these men, fundamentally opposed in principle, were without a party; none offered themselves to the people on a declaration of elemental principles; each submitted himself on his personality alone. Thus, in the absence of party and principles, purely personal politics entered in, and Monroe was embarrassed by personal feuds and factions that served only for the confusion of the people.

The fight in 1824 was between men, not principles or parties. Jackson led the poll, but not having a constitutional majority, the decision went to the House of Representatives which had to make a choice between the three highest in the poll, Jackson, Adams, and Crawford. The intrigues in the caucus were not inspiring. When Clay, who ranked fourth, threw his votes to Adams and out of gratitude, let us hope, was made Secretary of State, it was inevitable that the cry of "corrupt bargain" would be raised. The whole proceeding was undignified and indecent, and the charges and countercharges and the vituperation that ensued was a sad reflection on republican institutions. This disgusting exhibition throws a white light on government by personalities and not by parties.

Out of it all emerges one glaring fact—that personal politics is a mockery of democracy.

III

At the time of Jackson's election all men posed as members of the party of Jefferson, and a democracy with but one party is as dangerous as one with none. The totalitarians tolerate but one party and outlaw all others. During the first years of the republic there was but one definite political party with no organized opposition. It was a government party; and when Jefferson organized a party of opposition it is not surprising that, as in totalitarian states, the new party was denounced as "factious" and "subversive"—the favorite epithets of fascism and communism.

The party of Jefferson was swept into power by the people. The Federalists, after several attempts to regain power, gradually petered out; the old Hamiltonians infiltrated into the party of Jefferson; and to all outward seeming, we again had but one political party. But the Federalists, posing as Jeffersonians, were Hamiltonians still. It was the old story of the Trojan horse.

In the absence of party controversy, there was among the mass of the people a diminishing interest in public affairs. Political contests were between men, not principles, and the effect was destructive of the democratic process. Most conspicuous among the great contributions of Jackson to the welfare of the nation and to democratic institutions was his restoration of party government, making possible the determination of elections on announced principles and policies. He drove out the Trojan horse of Federalism by the creation of a party militantly Jeffersonian; the Federalists who had sneaked in went out to form the Whig party, and from that day to this we have had party government in America.

Jackson had been swept into office by the rising of the common people who constitute the overwhelming mass of the electorate. His mission was to govern in their interest—which was the real interest of the nation. But this great mass was without organization, discipline, or direction, and his mission was to give it what it lacked. In the bitterness of his defeat, Henry Clay had declared war on the Jackson administration within three weeks of the inauguration, and under these conditions the political party pledged to the support of the administration came into existence. Jackson's own words on the character and purpose of a political party were, "To give effect to any principle, you must avail yourself of the physical force of an organized body of men. This is true alike in war, politics or religion. You cannot organize men in effective bodies without giving them a reason for it. And when the organization is once made, you cannot keep it together unless you hold constantly before its members why they are organized."

IV

The purpose of this lecture is to show the methods through which he organized a party, how he gave its members a reason for its organization, and how he kept the reason constantly before them.

The first challenge of his enemies came in their fight in the Senate against the confirmation of a few of his appointees to minor positions. No President after Jefferson had such an appreciation of the press as a support for administration policies. A few editors had rendered yeoman service to him in the campaign and had notably contributed to his victory. He wished to summon these to his side in Washington. He had submitted the names of Amos Kendall of the Frankfort, Kentucky, *Argus of Western America,* of Isaac Hill of the *New Hampshire Patriot,* of Mordecai Noah of the *Enquirer* of New York, and of Major Henry Lee, the half brother of Robert E. Lee.

The enemies of Jackson hated these men for the very reason he appreciated them. The Senate was shocked in its delicate sensibilities that mere writers, molders of public opinion, should be proposed for even minor stations. It appears that in those days the men whose brains directed the press were not eligible for the social register. One Senator referred to them contemptuously as "a batch of printers."

The opposition rallied to humiliate the President and insult his friends by a refusal to confirm their appointments. The reasons, when not merely nebulous, were simply absurd. Thus, Kendall was rejected because his pen was powerful, and he had exposed the peculations of some of the opposition, soon to be languishing in prison. Mordecai Noah was rejected because of his Jewish blood by men who had no sympathy with Jefferson's ordinance of religious toleration. Major Lee, a man of culture and capacity who had intimately advised Jackson at the Hermitage during the campaign and had rendered distinguished service in securing the release of American prisoners when in Tunis, was rejected on the grave charge of being too fond of women. And Isaac Hill was rejected because his cutting wit and searing sarcasm had lacerated and scorched some of the opposition. Then, too, he was roundly denounced for having made "an attack" on Mrs. Adams—the attack consisting of the statement that she was an Englishwoman, unfamiliar with American ways; and this from men who had poured forth their filthy lies on the spotless character of Mrs. Jackson.

These insults to men appointed to minor positions would be insignificant but for the major role these men were to play in Jackson's later battles.

This challenge to the administration was vigorously met. Kendall was confirmed on a tie vote broken by Calhoun in the chair; Noah was first rejected and then confirmed on a second vote, again by the deciding vote of Calhoun. Hill was refused confirmation, but this tormenting wasp almost immediately appeared in the Senate to take the oath as a member to meet his enemies face to face. But John Tyler, leading the opposition to the confirmations, was delighted. "On Monday," he wrote, "we took the printers in hand. Out of those presented to the Senate, but two squeezed through, and that with the whole power of the Government thrown into the scale."

Yes, for the first time in our history, an American President donned his armor and went forth to battle for the press and to lift the editorial molders of public opinion to the status to which they were entitled as the educators of the people. This "batch of printers" were to become the storm troopers of Jackson in the Homeric struggles that were to follow.

V

In the creation of a political party the onus has been put on Jackson for having introduced the spoils system into American politics. The exact truth is that the spoils system had very little to do with the creation of the administration party. The spoils system began in the first days of the republic when for twelve years the Federalist party dominated the public service which was literally packed, even to the courts, with Federalist politicians to the exclusion of their critics.

Even so, it is uncomfortably true that with the inauguration of Jackson there was an unprecedented clamor for place from his partisans. This was due in part to the fact that the campaign had seen the entrance of new men into politics who had previously been excluded from the polls by a property qualification. These men were militant, conscious of their emergence, determined to share in the fruits of the victory, and they were noisy and importunate in their demands. They dramatized their demand for place.

The aristocratic or snobbish drawing rooms of Washington buzzed with gossip and rang with laughter over the indecorous scenes at Gadsby's Tavern when Jackson reached the capital. In great numbers, like stampeding cattle, they charged into the tavern to make their wishes known, noisy, vulgar, and uncouth, many in muddy boots and jeans begging for a laundry. These were the new men from the hinterland and the jobs most sought were minor. But the fashionables of society were convulsed and grasped their pens to write embroidered letters home, chuckling as they wrote. When Van Buren, Secretary of State, reached the capital to be instantly encircled by strangers demanding jobs and pursued to his lodgings, he was appalled. When, after taking office and harassed by the demands for place, he found the importunities of applicants so enormous that he complained in social circles, the ladies of the opposition laughed gleefully behind their fans and passed the news around. When Samuel Ingham, Secretary of the Treasury, complained at parties of the precious time he wasted filing applications he had no time to read, the ladies nudged one another with their elbows and giggled their delight.

Aside from the applicants themselves the demand was raucous and reverberating from the men who had fought Jackson's battle. One of them wrote, "No damn rascal who made use of an office for the purpose of keeping Mr Adams in and General Jackson out, is entitled to the least leniency save that of hanging." The editor of the *National Telegram,* soon to join the opposition, was assuming in his paper that the supporters of Adams would naturally be replaced; and Ike Hill was writing a friend that "the barnacles will be scraped clean of the ship of State, most of whom have grown so large and stick so tight that the scraping process may be fatal to them."

This ardent Jacksonian reflected the feeling of many when he wrote of Jackson's enemies, "They have provoked retaliation by the most profligate and abandoned course of electioneering; the most unheard of calumny and abuse was heaped upon the candidate of the people; he was called by every epithet they could find, and the amiable partner of his bosom was dragged before the people as worse than a convicted felon. What sympathy do people of such a party deserve when complaining that the places which they have abused have been given to others?"

VI

The demand for patronage was beyond precedent, but it would be a mistake to say that Jackson had no sympathy with the demand for a change. The cautious, cunning, conservative Van Buren was alarmed by the demand for wholesale removals. Major William B. Lewis, always at Jackson's elbow, living with him on terms of intimacy at the White House, protested against sweeping dismissals as creating the impression that "government is only valuable on account of its offices." And even Amos Kendall, the genius of the Kitchen Cabinet, shrank from the pain of depriving men of place.

Yes, within limits, the responsibility must be placed on Jackson himself. When John McLean, his Postmaster General, sought in the beginning to stem the tide of proscription by telling Jackson that if men who had participated in politics were to be dismissed, it would have to include men who had supported Jackson, the old soldier gave him a long, cold stare, puffing on his pipe in silence. Then he broke the silence. "Mr McLean, will you accept a seat on the bench of the Supreme

Court?" And McLean, who had presidential aspirations, bowed himself upon the bench.

When William Henry Harrison, just arrived in Bogota as minister, was slated for immediate recall, Barry, of the cabinet, sought to reach his chief on the sentimental side: "If you had seen him, as I did on the Thames, you would, I think, let him alone." And Jackson, peering through his pipe smoke, replied: "You may be right Barry. I reckon you are. But thank God I did not see him on the Thames."

However, it would be wrong to ascribe Jackson's policy of removals to a spirit of persecution. From the first days of his administration he was facing the organization of a powerful, relentless opposition to his regime under the brilliant leadership of Henry Clay. He was an old soldier and wise enough to know that it would be culpable in a commander to enter into an engagement with enemy snipers in the rear. He faced a ruthless and unscrupulous opposition, and he knew his administration would be wrecked if he had to rely on enemies in office to carry out his policies. He proposed to meet an organized opposition with an organized army of his own. He felt that the people who had entrusted him with the responsibilities of administration would expect that no one would be left in a position of trust who was not in harmony with his policies. He knew what we all know, that no private corporation would retain in its employ any man unable to work in harmony with the announced policies of the board of directors.

An illustration of his thought is seen in the case of the Indian commissioner who was removed. A friend of the dismissed official sought to soften the blow. "Why sir," he said, "everyone knows your qualifications for the place, but the General has long been satisfied that you are not in harmony with his views in regard to the Indians."

And if he was removed, why not? Is a President forced by

the proprieties to surround himself with subordinates working against the policies of his administration? Even so, historians too generally have grossly exaggerated the removals under Jackson. He dismissed all political enemies from posts that were strategic; but he left most of the others undisturbed. The political proscriptions of Jackson did not remotely approach the proscriptions when Lincoln took the helm. The truth is, despite the exaggerations of the opposition politicians of his time, that the vast majority of jobholders were unmolested throughout the two administrations of Jackson. He left in positions where they could do no harm a majority of his political enemies. He even appointed known enemies to technical positions when they were conspicuously fitted for the work.

Look at the record. With 8,600 post offices in the land only 800 postmasters were dismissed. A year and a half after Jackson's inauguration, a majority of the officeholders in Washington were of the camp of the enemy. The removals in the capital were but one seventh of those in office.

Then, too, the critics of Jackson ignore the fact that the expulsion from office of not a few was overdue because of their corruption. When Tobias Watkins, a personal friend and appointee of Adams, was removed there was an indignant hue and cry of persecution; it dwindled to a murmur and then to silence when, within a month, the discovery was made that he had stolen $7,000 of the public funds. This martyr was arrested, proved guilty, and sent to prison. The collector of Bath, in Maine, was found to have used $56,319 of the public funds for his personal ends; the collector of Portsmouth was found to have been doing a lucrative business as a smuggler; the collector of Petersburg was found to have used $24,857 of the public money; the collector of Perth Amboy was found to have falsified returns and to have used $88,000 of the public funds; the collector of Elizabeth City was caught stealing $32,791 of government money, and he hurried to Canada for his health. During the first eighteen months of the administration it was found that in the Treasury Department alone, almost $300,000 had been stolen.

The purpose of Jackson in the so-called use of spoils was to surround himself in strategic positions with men loyal, not disloyal to his policies and to create a team that would work together harmoniously under his captaincy. The use of patronage in the organization and consolidation of a party, if not incidental, was insignificant.

VII

One must go far beyond the use of patronage to find the explanation of the political genius which marked the Jackson administrations.

Members of Jackson's official cabinet, aspiring to the succession, and thinking primarily of the effect of his measures on their personal aspirations, were not militantly devoted to their chief, and most of them cringed before his audacious measures. Even Van Buren, who really was his friend, was frequently in distress because of his manner of facing the realities. The one member of the official cabinet who had the fighting heart of Jackson and fought for his policies was Roger Taney.

Bent on the consolidation of a powerful political party adhering to his policies, Jackson therefore surrounded himself with men devoted to him personally, as well as politically, and possessing political genius of a high order. The old-school politicians for a quarter of a century had concentrated on the cultivation of powerful personages in politics, business, and finance, and on the manipulation of caucuses. With the emergence of the plain people, with an awakened civic consciousness, the new conditions called for new political methods and a new technique. Jackson's followers were the masses; his mission was to organize them into a compact army, disciplined, munitioned, and prepared to march on the command of the leader.

This meant that he needed men who understood mass psychology; who had the feel of the people and who sensed the hidden aspirations of the hitherto inarticulate multitude; who realized that the time had come when public men had to concern themselves with the small farmer, the artisan, the socially unimportant people of the crossroads and the hamlets; who had a gift for organization and a genius for propaganda. And these men he found, for he had an uncanny knowledge of men acquired by mingling with them in the barracks and on the frontier. These men, who with Jackson revolutionized the political processes of the republic, are known as the Kitchen Cabinet.

Since overly fastidious men, wrapped in the swaddling clothes of politics and wearing the blinders of prejudice against the common people, have frowned upon these men as vulgar and violent, it is important to the student to know something of their character and the contribution of each to the creation and consolidation of a party that has continued without interruption for much more than a century.

VIII

During the campaign of 1828 Major William B. Lewis of Tennessee left his comfortable plantation and his treasured library to the management of his overseer to join Jackson at the Hermitage as an intimate adviser. He was to remain at Jackson's side for eight years, lodged in the White House. He was the first of the Kitchen Cabinet to appear in the capital. His status was different from that of the others. The others, while idolaters of Jackson the man, were militant supporters and advisers primarily because they were in complete sympathy with his policies. Lewis, more cautious and conservative than the others and sometimes doubting the wisdom of some of the policies, was inspired almost wholly by his utter devotion to the very human being he had known under the trees of the Hermitage. He was, however, a clever manipulator of men. Unlike the others, he was not a molder of policies nor the architect of programs. In the serene seclusion of the room he occupied in the White House he developed a genius in gauging public sentiment and in estimating the strength of the crosscurrents of public opinion. He had a special gift, developed if not inherent, for analyzing men and uncovering hidden motives. He, more than any of the others, frequented the halls of Congress observing the strategy of the enemy, and at night he and Jackson sat before the fire smoking their pipes while he gave his chief the result of his observations and conclusions. His value is measured by the advice Jackson gave Polk years later when he assumed the presidency: "Keep William B. Lewis to ferret out and make known the plots and intrigues hatching against you."

In a sense, he was a foil for Jackson. Where the President was prone to act on impulse, Lewis was deliberation itself; where Jackson was a fighter and often moved by personal prejudices, Lewis was tolerant in spirit and acted as a curb; and while Jackson was sometimes rash and impetuous, Lewis was always prudent.

Through voluminous correspondence he made and continued contacts with men of every degree in every little village of the hinterland until he knew precisely where each could be used when needed. His card index system, now commonplace, was perhaps the first ever used by an American politician. If action was required in some remote village, calling for some special quality, he knew to whom to send the instructions.

His relations with Jackson were very similar to those of

Louis Howe with Franklin D. Roosevelt. These men were loyal to the policies and ambitions of their chiefs, but their devotion was mostly for the man they loved.

IX

The supreme genius of the Kitchen Cabinet was Amos Kendall. He was a New Englander by birth and education. When very young, he found employment with Henry Clay at Ashland as the tutor of his children for $300 a year and the free use of the statesman's library. He began a journalistic career as the editor of a Kentucky paper, and his editorials, unlike those of his contemporaries, were constructive, reasoned, and free from vulgar abuse; it is significant that he specialized on banking and currency. Later, as editor of the Frankfort *Argus,* he made it a journal of power and distinction.

He developed a genius in polemics. His wit was biting. His style was elegant without being insipid. Far more than most editors of the hinterland at the time, he followed keenly and discussed international affairs with knowledge and penetration. He waged a campaign for free public schools. He assailed the national bank as unconstitutional and as possessing too much power. Though at first devoted to Henry Clay, he went over to Jackson in the campaign of 1828; and when Kentucky gave its electoral vote to Jackson, he asked and secured permission personally to carry it to Washington, and it was then that Jackson met him for the first time.

With his intuitive knowledge of men, Jackson saw his potentialities at a glance. To keep him in Washington, he made him fourth auditor of the Treasury, and while he efficiently discharged his duties, uncovering and denouncing numerous peculations, he so systematized his labor that he could devote most of his time to the politics of the administration.

Van Buren, who also could estimate men at a glance,

foresaw his influence and sought an introduction, and soon Kendall had become more powerful behind the screen than any member of the official cabinet. MacDonald, the historian, was to describe him years later as "a man of remarkable administrative power." Senator Foote of Mississippi was to describe him as "one of the most remarkable men in America" and as "discoursing upon the gravest and most important questions with a profundity and power which left a lasting impression." When Harriet Martineau, the brilliant English bluestocking, was in Washington, she found him "the moving spirit of the Administration, thinker, planner, doer, but all in the dark—work done of goblin-like extent and with goblin speed—undoubtedly a great genius."

He enveloped himself in a cloak of mystery. His health was not robust and his appearance in society was infrequent. But when this man of mystery appeared in a drawing room, his extremely sallow complexion, snow-white hair, and weary eyes concentrated all attention upon him. He figured conspicuously in the gossip of the drawing rooms where he was looked upon as secretive, as indeed he was, and as audacious in his methods. It was believed that he was the author of many of Jackson's state papers, and he was of not a few. He seldom appeared at the Capitol, and a member of Congress serving his fifth term did not see him once.

He was the Gray Eminence of the Jackson administration.

X

Quite a different member of the Kitchen Cabinet was Isaac Hill of New Hampshire. He, like Kendall, appeared in Washington for the inauguration. As the pugnacious editor of the *New Hampshire Patriot,* his career had been one of storm and stress. Indeed, his life had been in many ways a tragic drama. Though not the intellectual equal of Kendall, he was a master phrasemaker and for years his satiric and witty barbs had penetrated the hides of political opponents who took their revenge in indecent personal abuse. During the Jefferson administration he had bitterly attacked the Federalist secession movement with a battle-ax in 1808, and he was a thorn in the side of the dying party at the time of the Hartford Convention. So deadly were his blows that this crippled man was physically attacked and beaten by a Federalist gang in the streets of Concord. Because of the insanity of his father in his last days, the Federalist papers made merry over the tragedy, and they found amusement in the fact that Isaac was crippled.

Far off at the Hermitage, Jackson and Lewis had chuckled over the wit and savage denunciations of the *New Hampshire Patriot* throughout the campaign of 1828; and when the editor appeared at Gadsby's to greet his hero before the inauguration, he was not a stranger. Greeting him warmly, Jackson laughingly recalled and quoted from memory many of his visitor's quips.

He was in hearty accord with Jackson's democratic crusade, but he had reasons for his hatred of Jackson's enemies in his own bitter memories. The Yankee editor who shook the hand of Jackson that day was far from prepossessing. He was not only small, but crippled, and he appeared at Gadsby's dressed plainly as a working man; but Jackson did not judge men by their physical appearance or their dress. The venemous hatred of Jackson's enemies against the wasp of New England endeared him to Old Hickory. He had been a stalwart supporter of Jefferson, had denounced the Federalists' treasonable violation of the embargo, and had made the *Patriot* a power throughout New England. James Buchanan, on the floor of the Senate long afterwards, was to say that he had never known a man with a wider range of information on the United States. But the simulated contempt of the Federalists has been reflected in some pro-Federalist historians through all the intervening years.

The little crippled giant wore the hatred of the Federalists as a badge of honor. When his shafts struck home and his victims cried out, he clapped his hands ecstatically and exclaimed, "I have hit them, for they flutter." In the council room of the Jacksonians he was a power. In the Senate he attacked Jackson's foes with the ferocity of a swarm of angry bees, covering them with stings. At the close of Jackson's administrations he was overwhelmingly elected governor of New Hampshire, and he made one of the greatest executives that commonwealth has ever known.

XI

With Kendall, Hill, and Lewis in Washington the other member of the Kitchen Cabinet had not yet reached the scene of combat. Henry Clay had made his slashing attack on the Jackson administration before there was an administration policy to attack. It came from the injured vanity of Clay, from the bitterness of his humiliation, and it was personal. That early, it was common knowledge that he was bent on the organization of a robust party of opposition. It was known that he planned the acquisition of newspapers to carry on the attack. No one since Jefferson had such an appreciation of the importance of the press as Jackson, and the need for an administration organ was immediately manifest.

One memorable day Jackson sat down with Kendall, Lewis, and Hill to discuss the launching of a newspaper. The Gray Eminence urged the selection of Francis P. Blair, successor to Kendall on the Kentucky *Argus,* as the editorial director. Jackson recognized the name. He had been impressed with Blair's powerful editorial against nullification in the *Argus,* and that day the fourth man in the Kitchen Cabinet was summoned to Washington.

The man who appeared at the White House, beloved by Kendall, was disappointing to the fastidious Lewis. The brilliant college student, the erudite lawyer who did not practice, the master of polemics, was not reflected in the frail figure of the short, slender man, poorly garbed and with an impediment in his speech. His shyness gave no indication of the warrior spirit within the shabby clothes. Jackson saw through the clothing to the fighting heart of the man and instantly took him to his bosom. That day he was entertaining diplomats at dinner, and Blair was asked to stay. Ignorant of the nature of the dinner, he accepted; but when the other guests arrived in their gaudy uniforms sparkling with decorations and with their pretentious mannerisms, he hastily retired to a far corner of the room where Jackson found him; and taking him up by the arm he led him to the table and seated him beside him. From that hour Blair was to love Old Hickory.

He, like Hill, was ugly, yet he was of excellent stock; he had a fine, trained intellect, and he was a man of culture. As an editorial writer he had a rare gift of style that appealed to the intellectuals while delighting the multitude and maddening the enemy. His admirers compared him with Junius. He could be dignified without being dull and elegant without being flabby.

Though a stanch Jeffersonian, he had followed in the wake of Henry Clay but had turned against him on the "corrupt bargain" charge and against Calhoun on nullification. He accepted the invitation to head the administration paper which was to be a tremendous power for nine years; and thus, the Washington *Globe,* destined to become a powerful factor in the triumphs of Jackson, made its bow to the public.

XII

During the campaign of 1828, Duff Green of the Washington *Telegraph* had warmly supported Jackson, but he was an ardent supporter of Calhoun for the succession; and when Van Buren, whose presidential aspirations were unknown to Jackson, was given the first post in the official cabinet, Green turned violently against the man in the White House. It was at a White House levee, under the nose of Jackson, that Green confidentially informed newspapermen of the approaching rupture of Jackson and Calhoun and that arrangements were being made to get newspapers in strategic points throughout the country that would follow the lead of the *Telegraph* in an all out attack on the administration. Since the information was given "confidentially," it is not surprising that Jackson was almost immediately informed; a political secret is something that everyone knows. This threat by Duff Green hastened the founding of the *Globe.*

While Blair was arranging for his removal to Washington, Kendall and Lewis were perfecting plans, and these were complete when Blair reached the capital. A canvass had been made of the different departments to ascertain what portion of the public printing could be expected by the *Globe.* It is not remarkable that the State Department alone, under Van Buren, declined a commitment. That canny, clever politician, who thought it wiser to walk ten miles to see a girl than to write a letter, feared that the origin of the paper would be ascribed to him, and he wished to be in position to say that he knew nothing about it. No doubt he was right. Neither he nor any other member of the official cabinet would have much to do with the paper. It was to be under the absolute control of the new school of practical politicians in the Kitchen Cabinet.

The *Globe* appeared with the motto, "The world is governed too much." It was frankly dedicated in the first issue to "the discussion and maintenance of the principles that brought General Jackson into office." This was a direct challenge to the forces that were organizing against him.

The publication began in December, 1830, with two issues a week, but, as the controversy with the enemy intensified, a daily publication became imperative. This called for money beyond the reach of Blair or Kendall, but Blair was a man of resource. He summoned the supporters of the administration to subscribe for 600 copies at $10 a year, and the response was immediate. Thus, without drawing on the slender resources of the publisher the paper was put on a firm financial basis.

The slashing, sparkling style of the *Globe's* editorials, perfectly phrased and yet within the comprehension of the masses, made a profound impression. Soon, the opposition in Congress was thickly sprinkling the annals of debates with indignant denunciations, and these attacks drew from the Jacksonians a warmer adhesion. The paper had its place on the tables of Jacksonians along with the Bible. The powerful editorials of Blair and Kendall, copied in administration papers throughout the country, munitioned the men in the corn row and in the country stores. They consolidated and unified a political party, gave it intellectual stimulus and discipline, and made its adherents march to the tune it played.

Never had the need been greater. The three most powerful and picturesque orators in the Senate, Clay, Webster, and Calhoun, would soon open a savage fire on the administration, and the most important financial and commercial interests would be cheering them from the side lines. The mission of the *Globe* was to answer and counterattack and to awaken the mass of the people to a realization of their stake in the conflict. The pens of Kendall and Blair framed editorials that were sent to the papers in the hinterland to be printed in other papers as their own; and these were then reproduced in the *Globe* as an indication of public sentiment. This was something new in American politics.

The fame of the paper as Jackson's mouthpiece spread across the sea. When the *Globe* became critical of Russia apropos of Poland, Count Nesselrode, the famous foreign minister in St. Petersburg, summoned James Buchanan, the American minister, to protest against the unfriendly tone of the American press. The suave Buchanan replied that the American press was free and did not necessarily speak for the government. "Ah," said Nesselrode with a disconcerting smile, "but that does not apply to the *Globe* over which the Government exercises control." Buchanan reluctantly conceded that the *Globe* was often called the official paper, but, skirting the edge of prevarication, he denied that it was under government control. Again the disturbing smile of Nesselrode. "General Jackson," he said, "must certainly have some influence with the editor." And that was the general opinion in the United States.

And this opinion was amply justified. Every morning Blair appeared at the White House before breakfast to discuss existing conditions, to get Jackson's views, and then to hurry back to the *Globe* where his vitriolic pen dashed off editorials so skillful and devastating that Jackson's enemies were goaded to fury.

In the White House Jackson sat with Kendall and Blair puffing his clay pipe, commenting on their activities and plans, chuckling over the editorials and articles, but his suggestions were few. These men reflected his mind perfectly and stated his views accurately and with a force of language he himself could not approach, and he gave them free rein. He asked their opinions on politics and patronage and on international affairs. When asked for information on any subject, he would often reply with a chuckle, "Go to Frank Blair, he knows everything." Jackson was much closer to the titans of the Kitchen Cabinet than to his official advisers.

XIII

This was natural since these men, while not known as such, served the purpose of the national committees of the political parties of today; and it was the first national committee that functioned not only during the few months before an election but throughout the year.

It was these men who largely determined strategy. They helped frame policies. Without exception they were masters of effective propaganda. They had their agents in every nook and corner of the country on whom they could depend to do their bidding gladly and without question. The card index of Major Lewis made it possible to find at every crossroads the man eminently fitted for a specific task. They managed the campaigns and directed the fights—they served the purpose of a national committee.

This national committee had its headquarters in the office of the *Globe*. Thither, visitors from the country found their way with reports and for information and direction. Senators and congressmen of the Jacksonian party were usually in conference there with Blair. The office hummed with activity. The room was hazy and foul with the smoke of pipes that were not entirely sanitary. Gossip has it that the room in which these conferences were held was usually disorderly. It was a workshop, not a salon. And the master politicians were not Apollos or Beau Brummells. The crippled Ike Hill with his ugly visage, Frank Blair, uglier still, both men slight and in old clothes that needed pressing, and Amos Kendall, the Gray Eminence, whose sallow complexion, white hair, and drawn features hinted of ill health, were not models for an artist. Among these the master of them all was Kendall. He may be described as the national chairman of the national committee—and none greater has appeared in the more than a century that has intervened.

XIV

And so Jackson and his team of skilled politicians, who shared his convictions honestly and ardently, went into one of the most bitter struggles in our history perfectly equipped and fully armed. It was a new day that was dawning with a new generation remote from the Revolution—a generation of bold fighting men, independent, democratic, cognizant of their rights, and conscious of their power; and Jackson and the Kitchen Cabinet knew and understood the reactions of their minds and hearts.

They knew that the extermination of the Federalist party, followed by the misnamed era of good feeling, had led many to pose as Jeffersonians while in their hearts they were Federalists still. This, they knew, had subordinated principles to personalities and substituted personal ambitions for well-defined policies. Jackson and these practical politicians on his team rendered an immeasurable service to Americanism by recreating a political party which forced the creation of a party of opposition.

The Jacksonians created a party based on the fundamental principles of Jefferson; the opposition, not daring to afront the people with the name Federalist, called themselves the Whigs. "A grand name," said John Forsyth, the Jacksonian of Georgia, "and I am sure they will disgrace it." These Whigs were the Federalists of their time, accepting in large measure the discredited fundamental of Hamilton.

Jackson's conception of effective party leadership is well-defined. He thought of a political party as an army, munitioned with elemental principles, fighting for policies in conformity with those principles. He insisted on a party organization reaching down from the commander-in-chief to the most insignificant private in the most obscure hamlet and all undeviatingly following the program handed down from the leader.

Too much a soldier to enter a battle with enemy snipers in his rear, he demanded of his followers the utmost loyalty and the expulsion of the disloyal from the ranks. He had a soldier's contempt for the timeserver and the timid; he wanted no cringing cowards in the ranks of his army when he faced the foe. In his councils of war he listened to the various views of his lieutenants, but, once a decision was made, it was the decision of the party, his political army, and he demanded an unwavering adherence to the strategy agreed upon.

Just as in battle the old soldier concentrated his efforts on taking some specific place by storm, the politician—an old soldier still—entered his political struggles to concentrate on main objectives, and he brushed aside all extraneous matters with this in view. There never was any doubt as to the meaning of his orders, and the meanest private understood. He never fought with ping-pong sticks, but he entered his conflicts with a battle-ax, and he rode at the head of the column. He was the leader, and nothing was done by his subordinates without his approval and knowledge.

He assigned to his personal cabinet of practical politicians their respective tasks. He counted on Major Lewis for the management of men, for reports on the maneuvering of the enemy, and for close contact with his political soldiers down to the scullions and the cooks. He looked to Isaac Hill for the congenial task of harassing the enemy with his deadly darts of wit and irony. He assigned to Blair the important mission of munitioning his army with arguments and propaganda. But most of all, he depended on Amos Kendall, the greatest of them all, for an over-all supervision of the struggles; and much of the dramatic history of the Jackson administration can be written around the activities of this man of mystery.

XV

The most historic phase of Jackson's struggles was his war on the Bank of the United States against which Jefferson had warned. If the inspiration of his declaration of war did not come from Kendall, it came very close to it. Kendall had been warring on the bank for years before Jackson took the oath of office. That he had discussed the matter with Jackson who had reached a decision is manifest in the fact that Kendall wrote the editor of the New York *Courier and Enquirer* to begin attacks upon the bank since Jackson would attack it in his coming message.

When Clay tricked the bank into a premature rechartering of the institution to array it behind his presidential candidacy in 1832, he was met by Jackson with a fiery veto message that was a clear call to battle. That this veto message was phrased by Kendall and Blair there can be no doubt. Ideas had been contributed by Benton, Taney, and Livingston, but the actual phrasing to which men could march suggests an autographed manuscript of Kendall. And to reach the masses, the phrasing was as important as the ideas.

Kendall did not doubt that when the bank had recently added $28,000,000 to its discounts, thus multiplying its debtors and dependents, it had a political object—and unquestionably he was right. It was he who insisted on the removal of the government deposits—the most daring and drastic act in Jackson's war upon the bank. Here the Kitchen Cabinet played the major role.

Almost all of Jackson's official cabinet, all except Roger Taney, cringed before the audacity of the measure. Van Buren, always coy and cautious, was alarmed. One day at a dinner in the White House he protested to Kendall against the removal of the deposits on the ground that it would endanger the party's prospects in 1836. With his sallow face flushed, Kendall angrily rose to his feet, saying, "I can live under a corrupt despotism as well as any other man by keeping out of its way, which I shall certainly do." But when he added that if no action was taken he was ready to lay down his pen, it was Van Buren who apologized.

That Jackson was a bit apprehensive about the wisdom of the measure there is reason to believe. When persuaded of its necessity, the debate in administration circles centered on whether the removal should take place during the congressional recess or should await the meeting of Congress. Most of the official cabinet, including Van Buren, urged that nothing be done until Congress convened. Their purpose was to gain time in the hope that something would intervene to divert Jackson from his purpose.

Again the Kitchen Cabinet prevailed over the official advisers. Kendall and Blair insisted on recess action, and Kendall gave his reason: "Let the removal take place early so as to give us several months to defend the measure in the *Globe* and we will bring the people up to sustain you with a power that Congress will not dare resist."

Meanwhile, the opponents of the measure in the official cabinet were seeking to convince Jackson that the state banks, to which the deposits were to be transferred, would refuse to take them. "Send me to ask them," said Kendall to Jackson when the point was raised, "and I will settle that question." Not only did Jackson accept the suggestion, but he authorized Kendall to write his own instructions, and Kendall fared forth upon his mission. In Baltimore, New York, Boston, and Philadelphia enormous pressure was applied to divert him, reaching a climax in Philadelphia where he was boldly told that if he would abandon the fight on the bank it would mean a fortune in his lap. He did find the state banks fearful of the power of the great financial institution in Philadelphia, and this persuaded him all the more that its colossal power over money and credit endangered the liberties and economic rights of the people.

With Kendall on the road, where was Blair? Not only did Blair appear for conferences at the White House before breakfast, but he accompanied the President on his vacation journeys and now we find him with Jackson at the Rip Raps in Virginia urging early action. To camouflage the nature of the conversations he had inspired the press story that Jackson, who never rested, was at the Rip Raps enjoying a much-needed rest. While the public was pondering this deception, Jackson was working with Blair on the "Paper Read to the Cabinet" in which his decision would be announced.

This famous paper was not intended primarily for the official cabinet. It was not necessary to put the decision in writing. The practical politicians planned its publication in the press for the molding of public opinion; and here again we note the fine Italian hands of Kendall and Blair in the phrasing, though Taney had passed on the document before its release. The Jackson administration was the first in our history to take the mass of the people into its confidence as to its actions and motives.

The paper was read to the official cabinet; immediately it appeared in the *Globe* with appropriate editorial commendation, and speedily the *Globe* transmitted it to all the administration papers throughout the land. Thus, the people were aroused, and in the ensuing battle the heavy artillery of the *Globe* was turned constantly and with effect on Jackson's enemies, and in the molding of public opinion and in the awakening of the people it played a powerful part.

XVI

The enemies of Jackson in the Senate were making an all out attack on every phase of his administration. It was opposition for opposition's sake. It was to go to such extremes, even in international affairs, as to leave the United States, threatened with the guns of another nation, without a penny of appropriation for the fortification of our coasts.

Jackson was a great soldier, and he and the practical politicians near him knew that the best defense is a vigorous counterattack. They refused to take on a purely defensive role. And in attack the clever manipulators of the Kitchen Cabinet were in their element. One of their number, Isaac Hill, was now in the Senate by the side of the ever-battling Benton. And these practical politicians waged a never-ending fight. With their sensitive fingers on the public pulse, they took advantage of every opportunity to rally the people around their chief and against his most powerful enemy, Henry Clay. With the opposition intriguing in the Senate, they were addressing their appeals directly to the masses on the farms, to their prejudices, and above all, to their interests. And for the first time in twenty years the people as a whole interested themselves in public affairs. They gathered in groups in the country stores listening to the reading of the *Globe* or the papers that it served, and they discussed the maneuvering of the enemy in Washington, in the corn row, and in the homes. A giant had been born.

The Jacksonians knew that the high tariff views of Henry Clay were obnoxious to the farmers everywhere and especially in the South. Therefore, they made crystal clear the tariff views of their most dangerous foe. How long would the farmers accept the status assigned them as the hewers of wood and the drawers of water for the manufacturers of the East?

How long would the industrialists of the East use the instrumentalities of government to enrich themselves at the expense of the tillers of the soil?

But a better illustration of the strategy of these practical politicians of the Kitchen Cabinet fighting Jackson's battles is found in the manner in which, much against his wish, they maneuvered Clay into an unpopular position on the public lands. At that time there were more than 1,000,000 acres that remained the property of the national government. Hitherto, the proceeds from the sale of this land had gone to the extinguishment of the public debt. Now that the debt was all but liquidated, what was to be done with the vast empire that remained?

Thomas H. Benton, the administration's most valiant and powerful champion in the Senate, had long urged free grants to actual settlers who would redeem the wilderness by leveling the forests, bridging the streams, cultivating the soil, and building homes, schoolhouses, and churches. Here was an issue that throbbed with life.

Clay and the Federalists before him had preferred to hold this land from settlement to prevent the diminishment of the labor market in the industrial centers of New England and the East; their aim was to keep wages down. It was such a pet policy of the Federalists in the days of Jefferson that a Federal judge in a charge to a grand jury, shamed the people for wishing to leave the well-ordered society of New England for what he called the barbarism and anarchy in the benighted state of Tennessee. And a colleague of Clay in the cabinet of Adams had lamented in an official document the people's preference for agricultural over industrial pursuits. The strategy of the Jacksonians was to emphasize and dramatize Clay's position as to the vast empire of the public lands. Clay, too, was a wise politician, and pending the next election he planned to remain as remote from the discussion as he could.

What was the strategy of the Jacksonians? The disposition of the public lands could not be disregarded by Congress and in the nature of things the land question should have been referred to the Committee on Public Lands in the Senate for a report and recommendation. But, with an almost sinister cunning the clever leaders of the Jacksonian party had it referred, instead, to the Committee on Manufactures. Why? Because Henry Clay was the chairman of that committee.

Caught in the trap, Clay tried with persuasion, importunities, almost with tears, to have the reference made to the Committee on Public Lands without success, and he was forced to report a measure against the reduction in the price of land to actual settlers. Then the Jacksonians, under the militant leadership of Benton, registered indignation and moved in for the kill. Denouncing the Clay report as against the public interest, they now demanded that the disposition of the lands be referred to the Committee on Public Lands where it naturally belonged. The chairman of this committee, William R. King of Alabama, was a stanch Jacksonian. His report was written by the facile pen of Benton. It vigorously assailed the report of Clay and recommended the sale of land to actual settlers for a dollar an acre.

The issue was not only clearly drawn, but dramatized—the Clay report and the Jackson report were there on paper for all to read and ponder. One may imagine the sour grin of Blair, the chuckle of Hill, the unaccustomed smile on the somber face of Kendall. These men knew how the pioneers of the new states felt; knew that they wanted the wilderness redeemed by the inflow of settlers who would help in the leveling of the forest, the cultivating of the fields, the building of homes, schoolhouses, and churches.

From the *Globe* the two reports went forth to Jacksonian papers everywhere together with editorial propaganda, vigorous but simple, from the pens of Blair and Kendall. Again the Jacksonians profited because the practical politicians of the Kitchen Cabinet sensed the thoughts, the feelings, the prejudices of the masses, and they knew that in the South and West there was a growing resentment against the subordination of the farming interests to the manufacturers of New England, New Jersey, and New York.

XVII

The political policy and methods of Jackson and the Kitchen Cabinet—for it played the major part—not only established government by political parties but brought the mass of the people into the political picture. It made the party responsible, as never before, to all the adherents of the party, drawing them actively and responsibly into the formulation of policies and the nomination of candidates through the initiation of party conventions. They acted on the theory that democracy cannot function sanely unless all the people know the issues involved in a campaign, and it recognized the efficacy of the press in reaching the people with a discussion of the issues. They anticipated the modern system of party organization by reaching out to the individual in the far corners of the nation. They forced the acceptance of party discipline by demanding that with the adoption of a party policy it was the duty of every member down to the precincts to march as a unit; and that they who could not do so should leave the party.

Furthermore, the Kitchen Cabinet foreshadowed the party platform eight years before its adoption by party conventions. Early in the campaign of 1832, Amos Kendall, the intellectual who was a statesman as well as a politician, proposed to appeal to the minds of the thoughtful with a sober document in which the purposes and the achievements of the administration should be paraded in review. That able paper, the first of its kind, was the inspiration of the modern party platform.

Certain it is that the practical politicians around Jackson gave form to the organized system of party government and responsibility under which the American democracy has functioned intelligently for more than a century. If the people have not always acted intelligently, they have not blundered in the dark.

XVIII

The supreme achievement of these practical politicians around Jackson was in awakening the civic conscience of the great body of the electorate and in impressing them with the responsibility of citizenship. Had they failed in this, the bitter battles of the Jackson regime would have meant defeats and not triumphs. They faced, as ruthless foes, the challenge of the greatest financial institution of the nation with its control of cash and credit, its unscrupulous use of money, and its brazen resort to intimidation. And because of the bank they were challenged by the merchants of the cities who were at the mercy of the bank, by the manufacturers of the East demanding that special legislation pour profits into their coffers, and by the greater portion of the press. All these powerful interests knew precisely what they wanted and why they wanted it.

The Jacksonians in the Homeric campaign of 1832 championed the cause of the average man, the farmer, and the plain people of the villages previously unorganized, unconscious of their rightful stake in government, uninformed as to politics and legislation, and ignorant of their inherent power. As the crucial election approached, the problem of the Jacksonians was to reach their widely scattered elements; to inform them of their economic rights and dangers in language they could understand; to persuade them that they had a ligitimate interest in what was transpiring and to make this crystal clear; to inform them of the issues and their meaning; to reawaken their interest in the elemental differences in the two schools of political thought, as in the days of Jefferson and Hamilton; to organize them for united action; to munition them with arguments they could use at the country store; and to mobilize them into a militant fighting army behind the man in the White House who was their idol.

In the campaign of 1832 the new school of practical politicians behind Jackson aroused the common people to action as never before in American history. The farmers, their clothes stained with the soil, debated the issues with fervor. They talked politics in the fields, in the streets, about the fireside, and outside the church after Sunday services.

The enemies of Jackson could not understand this rising of the people. They tried to stem the tide with a barricade of moneybags of unprecedented proportions, and they tried to frighten the people with an economic reign of terror. In New Orleans a bank began discounting four-months paper at eight per cent "because of the Veto of the rechartering of the National Bank"; merchants supporting Jackson were refused credits at the banks; the Whig press announced that pigs would sell for $2.50 if Clay triumphed and for $1.50 if Jackson won; not a few manufacturers tried to coerce their workers with threats of dismissal; and the announcement was made that if Jackson should be elected no boats would be built in Pittsburgh or Wheeling.

The Whigs could not understand this new generation, but the Jacksonians did. The resort to bribery, intimidation, and coercion only served to fire the fighting blood of the masses. Through the pulsating propaganda of the *Globe* the people were convinced that this battle was their battle, that Jackson was being savagely assailed because he was their champion. And the response of the people rattled the dry bones of the old superannuated school of politicians.

All over the land the newly-awakened people made politics their business. They left the plow in the furrow, bade farewell to their families as though going forth to war, mounted their horses, and joined the huge processions of mounted men that moved with banners and shouts of defiance through the countryside from rally to rally.

When Jackson, returning to Washington from the Hermitage, approached Lexington, the home of Clay, a thousand horsemen met him a few miles out to escort him into the city of his rival. Their shouts beat like a hailstorm against the walls of Ashland, and as they rode, these men sang a song popularized through the *Globe*:

Here's a health to the heroes who fought
And conquered in Liberty's cause;
Here's health to Old Andy who could not be bought
To favor aristocrat laws.
Hurrah for the Roman-like chief
He never missed fire at all;
But ever when called to his country's relief
Had a ready picked flint and a ball.

And then the chorus rang like a roll of thunder over the countryside:

Hurrah for the Hickory tree
From the mountain tops down to the sea
It shall wave o'er the grave of the Tory and knave
And shelter the honest and free.

This popular fervor was incredible to the Whigs, but the Kitchen Cabinet and their associates understood. They had awakened the sleeping giant and given it a voice, and they had no doubt of the result. Soon, Hill was writing a friend to bet all he could on Pennsylvania and Ohio, that he himself was "on the turf," and that Benton in the West was "picking up all he can get," as was the son of Van Buren who was to make a fortune on his wagers.

XIX

This discussion of politics and politicians certainly is not beneath the dignity of history. For history, if understood, lifts the torch on the past to illuminate the future. From its pages one learns the reasons behind triumphs and defeats. And never have the lessons of history been so important as today when all society is in a state of change.

There are far too many half-baked intellectuals and parlor reformers today who are endangering the democratic system with sneers at political parties and politicians, unconscious of the fact that they are playing the game of the totalitarians of both the right and the left. These simple critics of parties and politicians have company, but it is a vicious antidemocratic company. They can point with assurance, if not with self-respect, to the elimination of parties and the damnation of politicians by Stalin, Hitler, Franco, and Peron with the view of grinding democracy beneath their heels. They are oblivious to the fact that conspiracies to wreck democratic institutions are invariably inaugurated with violent attacks on politics, politicians, and parliaments. The purpose always is to destroy the people's faith in their political leaders, to wreck confidence, to confuse the masses, and to pave the way for demagogues to mount and ride on the people's back to despotic power.

In a democracy there must be political parties or there is chaos, and if there are parties there must be politicians to lead and direct them; but the demagogues by denouncing all politicians as corrupt, can always find an audience among people ignorant of the lessons of history. There are some corrupt men in politics, just as there are bankers who embezzle, and business men who are crooked. If the white light of publicity was turned on every business transaction, if every business deal was subjected to the microscope as in the case of political actions, and the revelations given to the press, what would the result be? Because some politicians in the lower strata are corrupt, all politicians are corrupt; but no one suggests that because some bankers embezzle, all bankers are embezzlers, or because some business men are crooked, all business men are crooked.

Jefferson organized a party to save democracy; Lincoln and Roosevelt found the party system in full operation; but it was Jackson who found our political life disorganized and drifting toward the politics of clashing individual ambitions that leads to dictatorial rule, and through the organization or rather the establishment of the party system he made possible a functional democracy. Andrew Jackson ranks high among those who established the American system. He substituted principles and policies for personalities in the people's determination of the kind of government they wish.

And that is not least among the reasons why for more than a century the American people assemble annually on his birthday to pay tribute to the statesman and politician who, after many battles and bearing many scars, sleeps in the serene shade of the Hermitage he loved.

4

ANDREW JACKSON

The Homeric Battles of His Administrations

I

WHEN in the election of 1828 Andrew Jackson was borne on the backs of the people to the seat of power, a new day dawned in American history. The democratic philosophy of Thomas Jefferson became a reality. That ideology of liberty and personal rights to which Jefferson arrived through study and meditation was inherent in the nature of his disciple. In the wilderness among the pioneers, in the camps from which robust individualists and patriots followed him to victories, among the valiant men who cleared the forests and plowed the fields, he had lived the democracy he felt. From these associations had come his contempt for show and sham and snobbery, his distrust of the too great centralization of power, his hostility to monopoly, his challenge to the growing influence of wealth and privilege, and his utter devotion to the interest of the common man.

Jackson was the first of the Presidents to fight his way from actual poverty to power. His parents had migrated to America from Ireland to escape oppression and in search of opportunity. The death of his father in his fourteenth year left him wholly dependent on his own resources. At that early age when the patriots of the colonies began their march to independence, he joined the Revolutionary army. He saw his brothers fall in the fight for freedom, and sorrow killed his mother. Taken prisoner, he was struck down by the saber of a Hessian officer whose boots he had refused to polish. He was to have his revenge at New Orleans in 1815.

The War of 1812 with the British had been a succession of humiliations. Wholly unprepared to meet the onslaught of the enemy, the people saw the British army march triumphantly through the eastern countryside, its progress lighted by its conflagrations, until, in the nation's capital, it fired the Capitol, burned the White House, and forced President Madison to flight. Reassured by their easy victories, the British made their preparations to take New Orleans and the empire that Jefferson had brought under the jurisdiction of our flag. The expedition they prepared numbered half as many men as they had used in all the land beside. It included 12,000 veteran troops that had followed the sword of Wellington and 1,100 cannon. At its head was a veteran of the war in Spain and Portugal who, with Wellington, had driven the veterans of Napoleon back to France at the point of the bayonet. The defense of New Orleans and the inland empire it symbolized was entrusted to Andrew Jackson.

What were his resources? To meet the 12,000 veterans of Wellington and the 10,000 British sailors thrown into the fight, he had 6,000 troops including but 800 regulars. His army of defense was mostly composed of volunteers and militiamen from Kentucky, Tennessee, and Louisiana equipped only with the rifles, muskets, and shotguns they had used in the hunting field. But, between the trained, experienced, and well-equipped army of the invader and victory loomed the military genius and the indomitable will of Andrew Jackson.

He found the people of New Orleans unorganized and in

confusion; he brought order out of chaos with lightning speed. He ordered the cowards back with the scullions and the cooks; he crushed all who ignored his orders, and, when the defense was threatened by the interference of a judge and a district attorney, he ordered them under arrest. He promised "by the Eternal" to annihilate the foe.

On the memorable day of the battle he had drawn up his troops along a canal and, with dirt and cotton bales, had raised breastworks behind which these ill-armed men of the woods awaited the attack of the enemy. He paced constantly up and down before his men, imparting to them his own courage, determination, and enthusiasm. He ordered them to withhold their fire until they could see the whites of the eyes of the advancing foe. The British advanced confident of an easy conquest. Within half an hour the battle was over; 700 who had followed the sword of Wellington and triumphed over the army of Napoleon were dead, 1,400 were wounded before the fire of the sharpshooters of Kentucky and Tennessee, 500 were prisoners, and the enemy retreated in a disorderly panic. One of the most important military victories in American history had been won.

If true that the treaty of peace had been signed at Ghent before the battle, it is equally true that this was unknown when Jackson met and conquered the enemy, and quite as true that if the battle of New Orleans had not been fought and won, the story of the War of 1812 would have been humiliating to American pride. There, from behind the cotton bales of New Orleans, Andrew Jackson restored American confidence and wrote with his sword a glorious page in the history of American valor. And he had done something else, more personal to him—he had revenged himself for the brutal, cowardly saber blow of the Hessian officer whose boots he had refused to shine.

Less dramatic but equally brilliant was the part he played in the Creek War of 1813 when he commanded 3,000 troops in one of the bitterest struggles against the savages ever fought. The enemy was utterly ruthless. On the side lines, rendering assistance and encouragement to the Indians, were Spain and England. In that struggle it was the bravery, the clever strategy, the perseverance, the endurance, and the iron will of Jackson that prevailed. There is nothing more characteristic of this great man than the fact that, though weak and ill, suffering physical torture from wounds received in the gun fight with the Bentons, he sat erect on his horse and directed his men in the midst of the battle.

All this was known to the American people. Known, too, was the audacity and tenacity with which he had cut the red tape of diplomacy in the fight in Florida; and if he went beyond his authority and committed a breach of military etiquette, he also anticipated history.

His political career before his election to the presidency had been less impressive. He served a short time in the House and Senate and gave abundant proof of his Jeffersonian ideology. He resigned from both. The man of the woods and the fields was annoyed by the seeming futility of the dull debates.

II

Who was Jackson, the man whose historic battles made democracy a reality? The triumphant candidate who reached Washington to assume the high office to which the plain people of the nation had called him did not realize the popular conception of the great commander. His health was frail. He had passed his sixtieth birthday. A bullet received on the dueling field and not extracted gave him pain. A man of commanding stature, measuring more than six feet, he was very slender, and at first glance seemed old, though never weary. His long straight legs were thin, and though his shoulders were a little bowed by the burdens he had borne, he carried himself in public with pride and much grace of manner. His hair was white and stood erect, exposing a forehead that suggested the strength of his intellect. His blue, penetrating eyes, if small, were very much alive, and their disconcerting penetration was accentuated by the huge spectacles that he wore. The man's character was in those eyes, for, if they could flash with fury, they could melt with tenderness. The lantern jaws and the high cheekbones were those of a fighter. His chin was well-chiseled and his mouth was firm. His chest, which was his weakness, was flat. If, through the series of Homeric battles with men of great intellect, eloquence, and pitilessness, he never asked nor gave quarter, it was because of the iron will that overcame his physical weakness.

Now as to character. He had the simplicity of the true democrat who, in the beautiful valleys of the Tennessee and the Cumberland, had mingled as one with the robustious, sometimes boisterous pioneers who had no use for show or sham and were not impressed by pedigree, privilege, or wealth. He was entirely free of vanity or conceit, but he had an acute sense of personal dignity, and he met any affront to this with an implacable resentment which involved him more than once in an exchange of shots. In these personal controversies he was uncompromising. It was Thomas H. Benton who said that in a fight, "he went for a clean victory or a clean defeat."

His moral courage was equal to his physical, and of this there never was any doubt. Fear was foreign to his nature. Whether at the head of his soldiers, or among the perils of the wilderness, or on the field of honor, or in facing powerful enemies in the Senate with the odds against him, nothing made him flinch. Once convinced that he was right, he faced his foes, if need be, singlehanded. He was an intense individualist, subordinate to no man, dependent on no man's support. Some one has said that "the wolves hunt in packs, but the lion hunts alone." We have the real Jackson on the occasion at the Capitol when an assassination was attempted, and the frail old man, with uplifted cane, advanced on the assassin who held the smoking pistol in his hand.

His will was adamant and he faced all his fights with fierce determination. One day at the White House he underwent an operation for the extraction of a bullet and almost immediately appeared in the Blue Room to welcome guests with his usual courtliness and ease.

Living among the men of the Cumberland who met the perils of the unbroken forest with a smile of derision, he had learned the virtue of common sense which is often a good substitute for learning. He saw them create an organized society by their individual efforts, and no one could convince him that they who perfected that society were not entitled to its direction and control.

His appearance in Washington had been heralded by the snobs as the advent of a backwoodsman with no concept of the usages of society. In truth, he did not care for peacock poses. Admittedly, he was comfortable in his shirt sleeves, in old shoes, and with an ancient clay pipe on which he was usually puffing. But when occasion called, he could be as courtly as a courtier. When he arrived in New Orleans to take command and went about in old clothes making his arrangements, the elegant wife of Livingston was shocked at the idea of having him in her drawing room. "Wait until you see him socially," replied Livingston, "and you will be won over." The man who appeared that night in her drawing room, impeccably attired in his dress uniform, so impressed her by his grace of bearing and the charm of his conversation that from that hour, throughout her life, she was an idolator. When he appeared at Harvard to receive an honorary degree, and John Quincy Adams lamented the degradation of his alma mater by the honoring of an uncouth creature of the wilderness, his grace and dignity made a profound impression. God and nature made Andrew Jackson a great gentleman.

Perhaps it is not beneath the dignity of history to recall how he impressed one stranger who called at the White House. On leaving he told a friend that he had never met such a courtly and polished gentleman. A bit surprised, the friend replied that Old Hickory was a great soldier and statesman, but how, he asked, had the visitor found polish. "Well," was the answer, "he asked me if I would have a nip of whiskey. I told him I would not mind. He went out and came back with a jug of whiskey and a glass and handed them to me. Then he went to the window looking out, with his back to me, while I poured."

His honesty was proverbial. Not least among the reasons for the people's faith in him was his unimpeachable integrity. When in his earlier days he endorsed a note for a friend who did not honor it, he did not doubt his duty. He sold his first home in Tennessee with 30,000 acres to meet his obligation of honor without hesitation. It was then that he moved deeper into the country and built the log cabin he called the Hermitage, later to be replaced by the stately mansion which today is one of the nation's patriotic shrines. Such was his reputation for integrity that, when during a crisis in New Orleans, a draft of the Secretary of War was refused, Jackson was able to borrow $25,000 on his personal note without difficulty since his note was as good as gold in the bank.

That he was quick-tempered and could be violent in anger cannot be denied. He was much more high-strung than most men. But there was another side to his character—he could be as tender as a woman, and he loved children. Following a battle with the savages in which he had prevailed after a slaughter, he noticed a small Indian boy whose parents had been killed, and turning to an Indian woman he asked her to give it nourishment. "All his relatives are dead," she said. "Kill him too." Cut to the heart, he took the child under his protection and introduced him into his household where he was treated as though a son. His happiest hours in the White House were when playing with the children. A child's cry in the night would arouse him, and the old man would rise in the cold, go to the child's room, and walk the floor with it until it fell asleep. Benton has left us the story of having found him on a wet, cold evening seated alone before the fire with a child and a lamb between his knees. His passion of tenderness was as strong as that of hate. In his character is verified the words of the poet, "The bravest are the tenderest, The loving are the daring."

This man of the arena was happiest in his home. He was the soul of domesticity. One will search far to find a love idyl more beautiful than that of Jackson and his adored Rachel. He worshipped her living, and he never ceased to mourn her dead. The brutal attacks made upon her to serve the petty ends of politics all but broke her heart, and he never forgot nor forgave. The White House was lonesome without her. Every night he read from her Bible with her framed picture on the table beside him. Now that posterity shares his indignation and disgust because of the vicious slanders that were heaped upon her, his final tribute on the stone that marks her grave is too little known. That at his own grave bears a simple inscription: "General Andrew Jackson—born March 15th, 1767; died June 6, 1845." That was enough for him, but not for her, and he wrote the inscription for the stone of Rachel:

Here lies the remains of Mrs Rachel Jackson, wife of

> President Jackson, who died on the 22d of December 1825, aged sixty-one years. Her face was fair, her person pleasing, her temper amiable, her heart kindly. She delighted in relieving the wants of her fellow creatures, and cultivated that divine pleasure by the most liberal and unpretentious methods; to the poor she was a benefactor, to the rich an example, to the wretched a comforter, to the prosperous an ornament; her piety went hand in hand with her benevolence and she thanked her Creator for permitting her to do good. A being so gentle, so virtuous, slander might wound, but could not dishonor. Even death when he bore her from the arms of her husband, could but transfer her to the bosom of God.

A brief study of the character of Andrew Jackson helps to visualize him better and understand him in the bitter political battles that he waged.

III

The three most historic phases of the Jackson administrations were rich in drama. First, Jackson the nationalist.

Here he was engaged in a contest with John C. Calhoun. There is a background to their duel on nationalism that wrecked a friendship and probably prevented one of the greatest of Americans from reaching the presidency. Jackson had announced that he would have no one in his cabinet who had presidential aspirations. Calhoun, then Vice President, was conspicuous among the candidates; Martin Van Buren, though an aspirant, had cautiously kept his ambition undercover, and, without knowing of his aspirations, Jackson made him Secretary of State. This was resented by Calhoun though the breach then made was not too important.

The second incident had more deadly repercussions. Having heard that in the cabinet of Monroe the proposal had been made to discipline him for his action in Florida, Jackson had understood that his critic in the cabinet had been William H. Crawford. One day Jackson gave a dinner in honor of Monroe, then in retirement, and in the gossip across the table he was told that it was Calhoun who had proposed the censure. From that moment Jackson looked on Calhoun as an enemy.

These incidents had no direct connection with the savage battle with the South Carolinian which was to dramatize the Jackson administration. Up until 1816 the South Carolinians had been robust nationalists, but the tariff act of that year, in the interest of the industrialists of New England and detrimental to the economic interest of their section, aroused their ire; the tariff of 1828 was a more defiant piece of sectional legislation, and the conviction grew that the farmers of the South were to be immolated on the altar of New England greed. With the North predominant in Congress, not a few Southerners were persuaded that the ruin of the South was certain if the protective tariff policy to serve the special interest of the industrial North was to become the permanent policy of the nation.

Looming high above all the other statesmen of the South was John C. Calhoun. He had begun his career as an ardent nationalist, but the tariff policy alarmed him. He was a great political scientist and philosopher, a powerful orator whose speeches had the quality of Edmund Burke's orations, and he was a true patriot. He loved the Union but was convinced that the continuance of sectional legislation would end in the disruption of the Union that he loved. Out of his meditations came his doctrine of nullification—the right of a state to treat a law enacted by Congress as a nullity.

The struggle, now inevitable, was foreshadowed in the famous debate of Webster and Hayne in which the latter enunciated the Calhoun doctrine. The nullifiers formulated a plan to popularize their theory; they would take advantage of the first Jefferson birthday dinner in Washington to demonstrate their strength. The purpose was to capitalize on the popularity of the author of the Kentucky and Virginia Resolutions of 1798, which were designed to prevent the scrapping of the Bill of Rights and the establishment of a despotism. These resolutions were designed to force debate, to arouse the people to the danger to their freedoms. But—and here is the difference—Jefferson made it clear to Madison that they were not to be used in justification of armed resistance.

Jackson was invited to the dinner to create the impression that he, too, was sympathetic toward the nullification doctrine. No one doubted that he was a champion of states' rights; that he was hostile to the protective tariff; and that he loved the South. The twenty-four toasts on the program were all in support of nullification. With his usual insight into men and motives, Jackson sensed the nature and purpose of the dinner, and he sat down with Van Buren to determine the attitude he would take should the speeches be of the nature he feared. While the conspirators were felicitating themselves on the expected presence of the President, he was discussing with Van Buren the most effective way to dramatize his dissent.

The plan made, Jackson with Van Buren repaired to the dinner. The very thought of a conspiracy that would destroy the Union had aroused the lion in him. Always high-strung, he went to the repast prepared for battle. It was Old Hickory, the fighter, who sat down at the table and awaited events. He went "with feelings akin to those which would have animated his breast if the scene of this preliminary skirmish in defense of the Union had been a field of battle instead of a festive board."

Surveying the company, he found ample justification for his fear that mischief was afoot. The toasts to be proposed left no doubt. The congressional delegation from Pennsylvania left the banquet hall before the speeches; others, fearing a misinterpretation of their presence, quietly departed. The toasts began. Jackson in his chair sat impassive and immobile, an image carved in granite, his expression stern. At length, the speeches over, he was invited to propose a toast. Van Buren, who was short, mounted a chair to note the effect upon the company. Drawing himself up to his full height, he stood for a moment in silence looking at Calhoun; and then the silence was broken with a toast that made history and has rung like a clarion call down the corridors of time: "Our Federal Union—it must be preserved!"

It was more than a toast—it was a presidential proclamation; it was more than that—it was a declaration of war on all conspiracies to break the union of the states. He had thrown a bomb. The scene lost its festive air. The conspirators stood about in groups, their jubilation gone, and Jackson, giving no indication that he had done anything unusual, sauntered to the far end of the room to engage Benton in light conversation. This was in 1830.

In his home at Fort Hill, Calhoun finished his celebrated "exposition" announcing the doctrine of nullification, and the committee in the South Carolina legislature announced it as its own. It was the year of the savage presidential election of 1832, and Jackson was home at the Hermitage when he learned that the nullifiers had won a majority of seats in the South Carolina legislature. With his mind remote from the election, he hurried back to Washington fully panoplied for battle. When his friends appeared with news of his victory at the polls, he brushed them aside with mere thanks. Then he made one comment, "The best thing about this, gentlemen, is that it strengthens my hands in this struggle."

When three days later the legislature called the nullification convention for November 3, Jackson had already made his preliminary preparations. Secretary of War Cass ordered additional troops to Fort Moultrie; a secret emissary had been sent to Charleston to confer with Joel Poinsett, the leader of the Unionists there, for a report on the condition of the forts; and Poinsett was reading Jackson's words: "I am well advised as to the views and proceedings of the leading nullifiers. We are wide-awake here. The Union will be preserved; rest assured of this."

The convention met and adopted the nullification ordinance, and the legislature convened and enacted laws in conformity. While the Carolina Unionists met in convention and denounced the doctrine, Jackson sent 5,000 stands of muskets with equipment to Fort Pinckney and ordered a sloop of war with smaller vessels to the Charleston harbor.

Jackson has been called a rash and violent man, but, furious as he was, his mind was clear, his judgment just, and he took not a single step that did not meticulously accord with the Constitution and the laws. "The Union must be preserved and the laws duly executed," he wrote, "but by proper means . . . . The crisis must be met, and as far as my constitutional and legal powers authorize, will be met with energy and firmness."

Meanwhile, Jackson was at work on the proclamation he was to give the nation. He himself wrote the first draft, his pen spluttering over the paper. With Edward Livingston, who was to phrase it, he was in constant contact day and night. He was not happy. He loved his native state but thought the people wrong. He did not want to use force. One night he left his seat beside the fire where he sat puffing on his clay pipe, and going to the table on which was the picture of Rachel and her Bible, he wrote a touching appeal to the patriotism of his native state and sent it to Livingston with a note: "I submit the above as the conclusion of the Proclamation for your amendment and revision. Let it receive your best flight of eloquence to strike to the heart, and speak to the feelings of my deluded countrymen of South Carolina."

The day the proclamation was given to the nation, Jackson was like a war charger at the sound of the bugle call. His plans were made. When he received the acts of the South Carolina legislature he would go to Congress for legal and constitutional means to enforce the object of the proclamation. The Unionists under Poinsett were preparing to fight, but Jackson held them back.

The proclamation is a classic of American nationalism and ranks among the great state papers of history. Webster was delighted, John Marshall reassured, John Quincy Adams thought it a "blister plaster," and only Henry Clay refused his commendation. His reason is quite clear. As a perennial candidate for President he was angling for the support of the extreme states' rights men; and Van Buren was equally coy for the same reason though New York had acclaimed the proclamation with enthusiasm. Even so violent a Whig as Philip Hone was writing in his diary that it would "take its place in the archives of our country, and dwell in the memory of our citizens alongside the Farewell Address." Years later President Coolidge was to say that as a state paper the proclamation is "one of the greatest of any American President."

And now the issue had been made. Resigning the vice presidency in the crisis to take his seat in the Senate to defend his doctrine, Calhoun reached Washington. His people had crossed the Rubicon on nullification, but he had aroused them to a pitch he knew to be dangerous; many were out of control. At this juncture Jackson, moving scrupulously within the framework of the law and the Constitution, called on Congress for authority to use force if necessary. When the proclamation was given teeth by the force bill, no one longer doubted his grim determination to enforce the law and to preserve the Union.

Meanwhile, the administration forces, inspired by Jackson, had sponsored the Verplanck tariff bill drastically reducing the tariff and promising a further reduction still. He hoped to deprive the nullifiers of a weapon; most of all, he wished to prevent the spread of the nullification doctrine to other parts of the South. And here enters one of the ironies of history. Clay and the protectionists, against whose unjust tariff acts the nullifiers had arrayed themselves, were joined by the nullifiers to defeat the reduction of the tariff. When the bill had been mutilated by innumerable amendments, Jackson lost interest and the bill was dropped.

The debate on the force bill was one of the most brilliant and intense in our history since it revolved around the fundamentals. As the debate progressed, three brilliant Southern Senators championed the measure. There by the side of Jackson was Felix Grundy of Tennessee, statesman and forensic orator without a peer; William C. Rives of Virginia, statesman and diplomat, the finest type of gentleman in old Virginia; and John Forsyth of Georgia, the most powerful debater in the Senate. But Jackson was not satisfied with the course of the debate. The immortal trio, Clay, Webster, and Calhoun, had not yet spoken. He knew that from Clay nothing could be expected, and that from Calhoun would come one of his greatest and most powerful speeches. He knew that the one man qualified to cross swords with the great Carolinian was Webster. With Jackson action followed close on thought. One day the carriage of Livingston drew up at the door of Webster's lodging. The great orator was asked to enter the debate and reply to Calhoun. More, he was invited to assume the leadership on the floor and to offer any amendments he thought fit and proper. The invitation from Jackson appealed not only to his patriotism but to his vanity, and he accepted. Had Webster maintained the relations he then enjoyed with the iron man in the White House, he might have realized his life's ambition for the presidency.

The speech of Calhoun was probably the greatest he ever made, powerful in logic, profound in philosophy, and moving in eloquence; Webster replied with one of his greatest orations, brilliant, closely reasoned, free from personalities and passion —and the final words in the great debate had been spoken.

Meanwhile, Calhoun had unleashed a force at home that threatened to go beyond his intent since he was convinced that, driven to the last resort, Jackson would strike with every weapon given him by the Constitution and the law. With a spirit of compromise hovering over the Senate, an appeal was made to Henry Clay by one of his friends, but not by Jackson, to propose a compromise on the tariff. Thus came the compromise of 1833. History should have made it clear that Clay's action was motivated less by a desire to save the Union than by his wish to save the tariff system. We need no better proof than the opening words of his speech: "I believe that the American system [the tariff] is in the greatest danger." Another Whig leader, John M. Clayton, was franker when he said he "would never surrender the tariff even to save the Union."

The Clay bill conceded less to the planters of the South than that of the administration which the nullifiers had scorned, but conditions had changed. Jackson, in the White House with legal, constitutional weapons in his hand, had sent General Winfield Scott to Charleston with instructions to repel any attack upon the forts. So, despite features of the bill that were repugnant to Calhoun, he accepted them under the duress of necessity.

He hurried back to South Carolina to urge the acceptance of the compromise and the ordinance of nullification was rescinded by a vote of 153 to 4. Jackson had killed nullification without firing a shot and saved the Union without a violation of the Constitution or the law.

It hurt him to part with old friends on an issue he thought vital; and it grieved him to be forced to action against a people of a state he loved; but looming above all else was his love of the Union he had taken a solemn oath to defend. His position was all the harder because he, too, resented a tariff policy conceived in the interest of one section to the detriment of his South. He, too, was a champion of states' rights within the Union. He, too, was shocked by the fanatic, irresponsible crusade of the abolitionists, but above all else was his love of the Union which he defended at a critical moment with all the energy and firmness of his nature while moving against its enemies, despite his fury, with a cold, calculating respect for the Constitution and the laws.

His action at this time and his proclamation to the people place him among the most militant nationalists the nation has produced.

IV

Just as in home affairs he kept the one flag afloat, in international affairs he unfurled it from the peak and gave it a prestige beyond our borders it had never had before. He served notice to the world that the young republic would no longer be snubbed by any nation on the earth.

He had chosen his Secretaries of State with rare good judgment. In Martin Van Buren he had an accomplished diplomat and statesman on whose loyalty he could depend. Suave, tactful, ingratiating, sensitive to atmosphere, and erudite in international law and affairs, he followed his leader and sometimes guided him. His loyalty was such that he left the cabinet in the hope that his retirement would smooth out the factional differences due to clashing presidential aspirations.

Edward Livingston, who succeeded Van Buren, came from an old, aristocratic family famous in public affairs. Behind him was a distinguished professional and congressional career as an ardent supporter of the democracy of Jefferson. He had achieved international renown with his codification and reform of criminal law in Louisiana, and his work had been applauded by Jeremy Bentham, Louis Kossuth, the czar of Russia, and the king of Sweden. He had stood with Jackson behind the cotton bales in New Orleans. His character and associations had equipped him for the high post to which he was called on the resignation of Van Buren.

Louis McLane, who succeeded Livingston, had been conspicuously successful in the Senate and as minister to England. He was a natural diplomat, cautious, conciliatory, and yet firm and persistent in pursuit of his object. His ambition for the presidency and his innate conservatism which clashed with the bank policy of his chief created a cleavage, but in the international field he was militantly loyal. He reorganized the foreign service and put it on a better working basis than it had ever been before.

He was succeeded by John Forsyth of Georgia, a man of great ability, a persuasive orator whose voice was music, and the ablest debater in the Senate of Clay and Webster. It has been said of him that "as an impromptu debater to bring on an action or to cover a retreat, he never had his superior." His diplomatic papers were beyond criticism, forceful and yet couched in dignified phrasing. As minister to Spain he made progress in negotiating for the purchase of Florida. His personality was charming, his popularity unbounded by party lines, his manner courtly, and though ingratiating among friends he was haughty in the face of a foe. Even John Quincy

Adams, who loved few men, admired him and thought him eminently fair.

With these able, clever, and reasonably cautious men beside him, Jackson was brilliantly successful in international affairs, and historians hostile to his domestic policies have unanimously accorded him high place in the management of our foreign relations.

It was he who negotiated our first treaty of commerce with Turkey. The trade in the Near East and the Far East was rapidly expanding. The possibilities of the future loomed large, and Jackson had vision. He sought a permanent arrangement that would give free passage for our merchant ships to and from the Black Sea. He looked beyond today to tomorrow when this would provide a profitable market for our growing industries. These negotiations were maddeningly deliberate, for the East had always suspected the motives of the West, but the impatient Jackson, holding his eagerness in check, pressed the negotiations discreetly, won the confidence of the Turks, and, in the end, had negotiated a treaty of such importance that it became the basis for our commercial relations with Turkey for nearly a full century. Here he broke new ground and built a monument to his diplomacy.

Previous administrations had vainly sought a settlement with England that would open the ports of its West Indian possessions to American vessels without discrimination. These ports had been practically closed to us since 1783. During the administration of Monroe our vessels were permitted to carry products to the West Indies but only on the payment of colonial tariffs and with a discriminatory duty of ten per cent in favor of the British ships. We, in return, had opened our ports to British ships from the West Indies but with the imposition of a differential tonnage charge of one dollar a ton as well as a differential duty. Monroe had demanded complete equality between the American and British vessels in the West Indies as a condition for the relaxation of our own restrictions. This was the situation, with nothing accomplished, at the close of the Monroe administration. That of John Quincy Adams had pursued the same object and with as little success.

Jackson determined to force the issue. He proposed a settlement, not through interminable negotiations, but through legislation. He promised to open the ports of the United States to British vessels from the West Indies by presidential proclamation if the British would open the ports of their colonial possessions without discrimination against our ships. When the British stubbornly refused this proposal, the real Andrew Jackson emerged with the declaration that unless the British receded from their position, he would urge on Congress the extension of the interdict against the British colonies in the West Indies to include all the British possessions in North America with provisions for a rigid enforcement. Confronted by this threat, backed by the well-known determination of Jackson, the British abandoned their old position, revoked their order-in-council, and opened the ports of the West Indies to American ships fairly for the first time in almost half a century. Jackson succeeded where Monroe and Adams had failed, and thus he settled peaceably one of the most troublesome problems that had harassed us for fifty years.

Then the Texas problem rose to challenge him. Here is shed unaccustomed light on the character of Jackson. Some historians maintain that he was the proverbial bull in the china shop, rash, violent, and prone to subordinate methods to achievement without scruple. He wanted Texas, but he wanted it by purchase from Mexico for $5,000,000. When an inept diplomat of ours who thought wholly in terms of money proposed to increase the offer to $7,000,000, Jackson refused. When the Texas Revolution began, this diplomat urged that money would be needed to facilitate negotiations. Jackson denounced the suggestion as corrupt in its motive and the diplomat as a "scamp." When the same diplomat proposed a loan of $5,000,000 to the revolutionists, guaranteed by a mortgage on Texas, Jackson refused. When Texas declared its independence and sent commissioners to ask recognition and ultimate annexation, with instructions to appeal to Jackson as "an old acquaintance and personal friend," they found Secretary of State Forsyth personally cordial but officially noncommittal, and Jackson said nothing at all. Finally, they were told that annexation met with favor, but that it would be possible only if done "with propriety."

Why this coyness? Jackson insisted that recognition should come first from some country other than our own since our recognition first would create the impression that our action was motivated by our intention to annex. In a message to Congress he even went so far as to say that the facts then known would not warrant immediate recognition, and that Mexico or some other nation should lead the way. Finally, he told the Texas commissioners that should Congress vote recognition, he would concur.

But sectional opposition had developed. The tables of congressmen were piled high with abolitionist protests. The last administration of Jackson was drawing to a close. Forsyth, the Georgian, thought the recognition should come under a Northern President—and Van Buren was certain of the succession. One month before Jackson's regime passed to history, Congress voted recognition, and Texas immediately approached the administration asking admission to the Union. This was the state of affairs when Van Buren became President. Some years would intervene before another Tennessee President would definitely settle the Texas question.

The point here is this. Jackson had scrupulously avoided a

direct clash with Mexico. His purpose was meticulously to observe all the proprieties of international relations. He indignantly rebuked any suggestion of bribery. He respected international usage. He avoided any action that could be ascribed by other nations to an underhand intrigue looking to annexation. His diplomacy was wise and his hands were clean.

V

We now come to the most dramatic phase of Jackson's foreign policy which for the first time gave notice to the nations that the American republic would tolerate neither insult nor condescension from any country in the world.

After the passing of Napoleon the nations that had suffered from his spoliations submitted their claims for settlement and had these claims allowed. Those of the United States had been treated with indifference and a supercilious contempt. Madison, Monroe, and Adams had tried in vain to force a settlement. Outraged by the neglect or indifference, Jackson, early in his administration, determined to force the issue and compel the same consideration of our claims as had been accorded to European nations.

His first move was to send as minister to France the accomplished William C. Rives of Virginia, a clever diplomat whose aristocratic social graces would not jar on the pretentious court of Charles X. His polite insistence had resulted in a treaty recognizing our claims which was on the point of being signed when the July Revolution of 1830 swept the Bourbons from power, and the reign of Louis Philippe began. Negotiations were begun anew. Louis Philippe recognized the justice of our position, and a new treaty was signed providing for the payment to the United States of 25,000,000 francs in full settlement of our claims. From the amount paid us, 1,500,000 francs were to be deducted to meet the claims of French citizens against the United States. In exchange for the abandonment of the French interpretation of a disputed article in the treaty of purchase of Louisiana, we agreed to admit French wines to our ports duty free.

Thoroughly satisfied, Jackson announced the signing of the treaty with the observation that "a source of irritation will be stopped that has for so many years alienated two nations that from interest, as well as the remembrance of early associations, ought to cherish the most friendly relations." The treaty was promptly ratified by the Senate and ratifications were exchanged in February, 1832. The United States immediately carried out its part of the bargain by admitting French wines without the payment of duty.

Twelve months after the exchange of ratifications the United States drew on France for the first installment of payments. Nothing was done in France to make the money available. Louis Philippe conceded that the honor of France was involved, but the chamber of deputies was not pressed for an appropriation. James Buchanan, passing through Paris on his way home from his Russian mission, was given an explanation of the delay by the Russian ambassador. He was told that the delay was due in part to the weakness of the government and in part to the cupidity of the president of the chamber of deputies. The king's position was weak. The monarchists hated America because of the Revolution, and the republicans in the chamber hated the king. In consequence the government was reluctant to test its strength in the chamber with an insistence on the appropriation.

When the chamber refused to act on the appropriation, Jackson's indignation flared. "By the Eternal" he would have action. He sent Livingston to Paris as minister with stiff instructions to insist on the honoring of the treaty. The king again gave solemn assurance, but this time the chamber defeated the appropriation. Livingston proposed retaliation by suspending the laws enacted to carry out our part of the bargain. Jackson refused on the ground that this would weaken our position. He told Livingston that "the true policy is scrupulously to fulfill our engagements and rigidly to exact a similar performance from others."

His indignation was cooled by the announcement that the French were sending a vessel carrying instructions to the French minister in Washington with satisfactory explanations. Pending the arrival of the promised explanations, Livingston was instructed to inform the monarchy that Jackson expected him to convoke the chamber at an early date to make the appropriation. He learned that the king could not call an extra session on a matter the French clearly thought trivial.

The crisis swiftly approached. It was at this juncture that Livingston, acting on a hint from either the king or Lafayette, reported to Jackson that only a manifestation of strong feeling in America would force the chamber to a realization of Jackson's grim determination. Three times the chamber had refused to honor the treaty that France had signed. The vessel from France arrived, but the explanations offered by the French minister were wholly unsatisfactory; and Livingston pessimistically reported that in his opinion the king would not insist on the appropriation and that the chamber would not act.

This contemptuous indifference, a striking contrast to the treatment accorded the claims of European nations, put Old Hickory on his mettle. When he sat down to the preparation of his message to Congress, his advisers, cognizant of his fury, were alarmed. He wrote his message in a white heat of anger and sent it to the public printer. Then, with his timid friends, he sat listening to the reading of the proofs. "Read that again," he said sharply. Again the paragraph which his advisers had moderated without his knowledge or consent was read. "That, sir, is not my language," he shouted. "It has been changed and I will have no other expression of my meaning than my own words." And taking up his pen he rewrote the paragraph and made it stronger than before. Then, with his embarrassed friends about him, he handed it to the printer with the warning that if one syllable was changed in the next proof submitted, it would be at his peril.

This message was mostly a calm recital of the facts, but it ended with the request for authority to make reprisals if nothing was done in Paris. Even this was phrased in such a way as to leave the French an outlet for their dignity: "Such a measure ought not to be considered by France as a menace. Her pride and power are two well-known . . . and preclude the necessity of a declaration that nothing partaking of the character of intimidation is intended by us."

The sternness of the message in which the people saw the shimmering of Jackson's sword made a popular appeal, but the Whigs, ready to sacrifice their country's dignity and interest to their prejudice and hate, made their plans to discredit their President in the face of the foe. When the message reached France, it was hurried to Livingston by courier at two in the morning. He was stunned by its strength, but he believed it would have effect. In delivering it to the minister of foreign affairs, he pointed out that the message was addressed from one branch of the American government to another, and not to France; and then he shifted to the offensive with the observation that it was most unfortunate that the convoking of the chamber had been so long delayed. Finally, it had been called, but this could not have been known to Jackson when he wrote the message.

The French chamber and press roared with indignation and menaces. "The long sword of France can reach far," shouted one deputy. Another said that if the Senate supported

Jackson, the heroes of Navarino and Algiers would show that France knew the way to Washington as well as the British. They sneered at the arrogance of the little nation. The French minister was recalled and Livingston was told that he could have his passports on request. That careful diplomat made no request, preferring that any initiative looking to a rupture should come from France. But Jackson, now in full fighting armor, ordered him to leave France and turn the legation over to Thomas Barton, the chargé.

The Whigs under Clay and Webster were delighted with the reaction in Paris, with the sneers and insults heaped upon the President of their country.

At this critical stage their official organ expressed the hope that the French would understand that Jackson had acted on his own and without the support of public opinion or of the Senate. They hurriedly packed the Senate Committee on Foreign Affairs in the interests of the enemy. From this came the report of Clay refusing authority to Jackson to make reprisals, and 20,000 copies were ordered printed for distribution. The report actually suggested that the French might be satisfied with an "explanation" or apology from Jackson. The resolution, based on Clay's report, was passed by a party vote.

Before the controversy reached the House of Representatives, offers of military service were pouring in on Jackson. And here unfolds one of the most thrilling dramas in American history; it concerns John Quincy Adams, the most finished diplomat in all our annals. Petty in minor things, often prejudiced, always irritable, but of heroic stature when patriotism or principle was involved, he had left the White House in a huff, refusing to stay to greet the man who had defeated him. At the unfolding of this drama, this former President was a Whig member of the House. He was not even on speaking terms with Jackson. But he understood the language of vibrant patriotism when he heard it—and he had heard it in the message of his successor. He knew that the vital interest and the honor of the nation were at stake. He favored the continuance of negotiations, but if they failed he was ready for the hazard of war. The pledge of France had been given, and he asked "whether we shall suffer the nation that made the treaty to violate it. Permit it and every nation will consider itself at liberty to sport with all treaties that are made with us."

And then, with the astonished Jacksonians bowing to the militant leadership of Adams, the old man rose to the heights, to the consternation of the Whigs and the jubilation of the Jacksonians, when he declared, "Whatever may be said of the imprudence of that recommendation, the opinion of mankind will ever be that it was high-spirited and lofty, and such as became the individual from whom it emanated. I say it now, and I repeat, that it is the attitude which the Chief Magistrate will bear before the world, and before mankind, and before posterity."

Then, turning upon his fellow partisans who were loud in their praise of France, the old man asked, "Whence come these compliments to France? Is it because she has refused the payment due us? Is it because she has violated her plighted faith? Is it from the style of the dignified debates where we are characterized as a nation of mercenaries where the basest and meanest motives are attributed to the American people—avarice, speculation and gain?"

This was the first act in the drama of Adams as the champion of Jackson. There will be another.

The Whigs now were skirting close to treason. The report was current that a French war fleet was headed toward American waters. Diplomatic relations had all but ceased. Congress was on the verge of adjournment when the administration urged on the House of Representatives an amendment to the fortification bill appropriating $3,000,000 to be used at the discretion of the President in the event of war during the congressional recess. It was the last night of the Congress. It would die at midnight. The House instantly accepted the amendment and hurried it to the Senate where Clay and Webster began a filibuster. Midnight came. Jackson, waiting in his room at the Capitol, put on his hat and returned to the White House. The Congress died, and with it died not only the amendment but the fortification bill, leaving all the fortifications of our coast naked to our enemies.

The indignation of the country turned upon the Whigs, and in the next Congress, Webster, in undertaking a defense of their action, went so far as to say that he "would rather see a foreign foe battering down the walls of the Capitol" than to agree to the amendment of the fortification bill.

The reply to Webster was made in the House. Again the Jacksonians stood aside, and Adams again took the center of the stage. As a great patriot, this was his supreme moment, and this was the most pulsating patriotic oration of his life—this reply to Webster. Referring to Webster's amazing declaration, "the old man eloquent" paused a moment for effect. Then he spoke: "For a man uttering such sentiments there would be but one step more, and an easy one to take, and that would be, with the enemy at the walls of the Capitol to join them in battering them down." The Jacksonians were on their feet cheering wildly, and James K. Polk in the chair was unable to restore order. "Thank God," the orator continued, "the people of the country have done homage to the spirit" of Andrew Jackson.

By this time the French were convinced that the American people were in dead earnest, and, taking their cue from the Whigs, they made the appropriation with the payment conditioned on an explanation or apology from Andrew Jackson. How little they knew the iron man in the White House! When the

French minister sought to present a note to this effect, John Forsyth haughtily refused to receive it. Barton, the chargé still in Paris, was instructed to inquire if the money would be paid. If a definite date was given, he was to remain; if not, he was immediately to lock the legation and return. Just before this Livingston had warned the French government that if an attempt were made to force an explanation or apology it would be met "by the undivided energy of the nation." On his return to New York from Paris Livingston had been greeted by a great multitude of cheering men shouting "no apology" and "hurrah for Jackson."

But the money was not paid. Barton returned home. In a message to Congress Jackson said that "the spirit of the American people, the dignity of the Legislature, and the firm resolve of the Executive Government" forbade an apology or explanation, and he called on Congress to "sustain the Executive exertions in such measure as the case may require."

With Jackson firm and unyielding as Gibraltar, England now came forward with an offer of mediation. With real Jacksonian directness and decision Jackson agreed to mediation, but with this condition—he accepted only with the distinct understanding that the result would have to be no apology and that the money due under the treaty would have to be paid. However astonished the English diplomat may have been, he controlled his features and accepted the conditions. And thus it came about, despite the partisan opposition to a legitimate demand, that the French spoliation claims were paid, and the world took notice as never before in our history that no nation, however powerful, would be permitted to sport with the dignity and honor of the American republic.

Never had the prestige of the United States been so high as now. Never again would any country feel at liberty to play fast and loose with its treaties with the United States. Generations later, John Fiske, the historian, would conclude that as a result of Jackson's battle "the days when foreign Powers could safely insult us were gone." Jackson had placed his country on a lofty peak, and there it will remain as long as the spirit of Old Hickory inspires our conduct in international affairs.

VI

As a nationalist Jackson had succeeded in preserving the Union. In the international field he had successfully served notice that the nation would fight, if need be, for the prestige and dignity of the republic. Yet, in a third field came his greatest service—his Homeric battles for the preservation of our democratic institutions and the subordination of money to men in the determination of national policies. Here his struggle was with the Bank of the United States.

This bank was born of the brain of Alexander Hamilton who despised democracy and sincerely believed that organized wealth should dominate the government and that governmental stability is assured when government is made a source of revenue to the powerful. Thomas Jefferson foresaw its ultimate effect and opposed its establishment. When it was created, Jefferson wrote Monroe that "we are completely saddled and bridled, and the bank is so firmly mounted on us that we must go where they will guide us." In a letter to Albert Gallatin ten years later, he wrote that from the character of the bank directors and their sentiments and from their press he knew the direction they were going: "Now while we are strong it is the greatest debt we owe to the safety of our Constitution to bring this powerful enemy to a perfect subordination under its authority." And that same year in a letter to John W. Eppes he wrote, "This bank oligarchy or monarchy enters the field with ninety million dollars to direct and control the politics of the nation; and of the influence on our politics, and into what scale it will be thrown we have abundant experience."

Andrew Jackson was an ardent follower of Thomas Jefferson when the bank was created by a narrow congressional majority. He believed, as Jefferson believed, that it was unconstitutional; and, like Jefferson, he knew that it would use its power through its control of credit and the liberal use of money to dominate the politics of the nation. Jefferson never altered his opinion, and neither did Jackson.

When Jackson assumed the presidency this moneyed institution, conscious of its power, had reached the height of its arrogance and condescension. The existing charter of the bank had five years to run. The issue was not immediate nor acute. The majority of the cabinet was not unfriendly to the bank; and the majority never were to be militant supporters of the bank policy of their chief. But close to Jackson were Amos Kendall and Francis Blair of the much-maligned Kitchen Cabinet of practical politicians, and these were uncompromising enemies of the institution.

It is not remarkable that in his message to Congress in December, 1830, Jackson should have questioned the constitutionality of the bank. In its original form it was a slashing attack. After its completion it was submitted for criticism to James A. Hamilton. In him we have one of the mysteries of history. He was the son of Alexander Hamilton, the creator of the bank, but he had renounced the Federalist party and had warmly aligned himself with its enemies. When he returned the message to Jackson, the reference to the bank was in a brief paragraph questioning its constitutionality and asserting that it had "failed in the great end of establishing a uniform and sound currency." Jackson accepted the change. However, word had trickled out that the message would be an attack, and some administration papers launched vigorous attacks upon it. But with the existing charter running for five years, there was a pause. In his message of December, 1831, Jackson merely referred to his observations in the previous message.

Meanwhile, Nicholas Biddle, the president of the bank, alarmed by the gossip, was writing his friends that the reference to the bank in the message was merely the personal view of Jackson without the support of the cabinet, and that it had not even been accepted as the position of Jackson's party. At this time Henry Clay was assuring Biddle that Jackson not only would not veto a rechartering of the bank five years before the expiration of the old charter, but would sign a recharter bill. Biddle, however, found his anxiety increasing when the vultures of politics began descending upon him with demands for money. Duff Green of the Washington *Telegraph* had applied for a loan of $20,000. It was at this time that Biddle began an assiduous cultivation of the press with the money of the bank, the government deposits.

After the second message Clay began to urge on Biddle an immediate application for a recharter, five years before the expiration of the old. Jackson did not favor a challenge to the bank at this time. He knew that the precipitation of the fight would inject the institution into the presidential campaign less than a year later. Even so bellicose a fighter as Benton would have postponed the struggle, but Clay was at Biddle's elbow urging action.

The bitter struggle that was to begin and continue for four years was on the demand of Clay, not Jackson. The reason is manifest. The popular orator of the Whigs went through the greater portion of his life hungering for the presidency. His nomination by the Whigs in 1832 was certain. He was seeking success at the polls. He knew that if the recharter measure was passed and vetoed by Jackson, the bank would be forced to fight and forced to pour its money into the campaign in his support. Webster, equally eager for a triumph over the man who had triumphed over the English, joined Clay in putting pressure on the bank.

Deeply disturbed and still reluctant, Biddle hurried to Washington for the historic conference with Clay and Webster. He found them still making their demands for immediate action, but he still drew back until the pressure took the form of polite blackmail. Did Biddle want to continue to have the support of Clay and Webster in the Senate? Then he must follow their advice. Again Clay gave his word that a recharter bill would pass, and, if vetoed, would be passed over Jackson's veto.

Thus, the bank fight was forced, not by the rash and prejudiced Jackson as some historians would have us believe, but by Henry Clay to serve his personal ambition. The bill was introduced. In the Senate it was referred to a committee composed of four servants of the bank and one Jacksonian. In the House the battle began with an attempt to have it referred to the Committee on Ways and Means, packed with the enemies of Jackson. That failed and the administration forces introduced numerous amendments followed by long speeches charging the bank with usury, with the issuance of bank notes by branch banks as currency, with the selling of coin, and with loaning government deposits to editors, brokers, and members of Congress.

Gravely alarmed, Biddle hurried to Washington personally to take charge, and at the Barnard Hotel he gave elaborate dinners to members of Congress who were singularly lacking in a sense of delicacy or decency. Biddle was no ordinary money-grubber. When serving as secretary of the American legation in Paris under Monroe, he had learned the ways of diplomacy. He was a real aristocrat as well as autocrat. He was elegant and graceful in manner, suave and highly polished, schooled in literature, scintillating and amusing in conversation; and his correspondence which was to reveal much to history was as rich in charm as in indiscretions. He was clever and unscrupulous in his methods. He entertained in courtly fashion in his home in Philadelphia and in Washington, and the members of Congress who enjoyed his hospitality became the nucleus of a bank party that looked with condescension on the chief of state. Through the earnest loyalty of members of Congress who were the beneficiaries of his bounty, he was better informed on congressional gossip than the President. But, like all dictators, he was vain, and, instead of concealing his power, he flaunted it in the face of the people. Having gone to Washington, he literally lived at the Capitol, and on July 3, in the year of the presidential election, he was able to report to his directors that a bill rechartering the bank had passed Congress five years before the old charter expired.

Triumphant until then, he concentrated now on an effort to prevent a veto; almost daily he had contact with his supporters in the cabinet. But Clay was eager for a veto that would force the bank deeper into the campaign of 1832. The passage of the recharter bill had aroused the ire of Jackson. The contest now was between Emperor Nicholas, as Biddle was called, and the President of the United States. "I will prove to them," said Jackson, "that I never flinch," and his veto followed close on the passage of the measure. That veto has been criticized as an incitation to class warfare, but Jackson had not invited the contest which had been forced upon him. However, he aimed to strike sturdy blows:

> It is to be regretted that the rich and powerful too often bend the acts of government to their selfish purposes. Every man is equally entitled to protection by law, but when the laws undertake to add to their natural and just advantages artificial distinctions, to

> grant gratuities and exclusive privileges, to make the rich richer and the powerful more potent, the humble members of society—the farmers, mechanics and laborers, who have neither the time nor means of securing like favors to themselves, have a right to complain of the injustice of their government. . . . Many of our rich have not been content with equal protection and equal benefits but have besought us to make them richer by acts of Congress.

The issue was then crystal clear as Jefferson had foreseen. The champions of the Hamiltonian theory that to make a government strong it must be made profitable to the powerful were in the saddle, booted and spurred. The issue that emerged was this—should the democracy of Jefferson continue or yield to a plutocracy? Should the economic rights of the common man give way to the domination of money? Should the democracy that triumphed under Jefferson end after thirty years to the Hamiltonian concept of society that Jefferson had crushed?

VII

Too few historians have seemed to realize that this was a contest on the fundamental principles of the nation. An embryo plutocracy had arisen, was in possession of leading newspapers, and had its cohorts in Congress with bank money jingling in their pockets. Even then Biddle had become the Emperor Nicholas. When he appeared in Washington, too many members of Congress flocked to Barnard's to get his orders; when a levee of the President at the White House collided with a levee of Biddle at Barnard's, too many snubbed the head of the nation to bow humbly before the head of the bank. Editors were now getting unsecured loans with the feeling that they would not be annoyed with demands for payment. At this time in the midst of the bank struggle Daniel Webster, championing the bank, wrote to Biddle, "I believe my retainer has not been renewed or refreshed as usual [note the "as usual"] and if it is wished that my relations to the bank should continue, it would be well to send me the usual retainer." This from Webster! Imagine the bank relations of lesser men.

Yes, democracy and the Jeffersonian principle of equal rights were in the twilight; the sun was warming the cohorts of plutocracy who at this time were nearer triumph than they had ever been before. But the voice of the people began to be heard over the clamor in Congress, and the bank could not muster enough votes to override the veto. This was as Clay had planned. The presidential campaign was opening, and the bank with its gold would be forced to move to his side with its moneybags. Suffice it to say that thanks to the immense popularity of Jackson and the brilliant strategy of the practical politicians of the Kitchen Cabinet, Jackson again triumphed.

But a battle, not the war, had been won; and Jackson, who believed in the extermination of the enemy, then launched his counteroffensive after the election. His personal victory had been won, but not that of the nation. The active participation of the bank in the campaign had been notorious; the bitterness engendered had been intense; and the bank was still in position to use the government deposits in a war upon the people's government. Jackson determined to pull its fangs by the removal of the government deposits. Most of the cabinet were opposed, some through fear and some through a secret partiality for the bank. When William J. Duane, Secretary of the Treasury and a weakling partial to the bank, procrastinated, he was summarily removed, and into his place stepped a fighting man after Jackson's own heart—the brilliant Roger B. Taney, a great lawyer and jurist, a profound thinker, and a man of unimpeachable integrity who for so many years was to sit in the seat of John Marshall.

This served notice that the struggle was to the death. Biddle sent a memorial to Congress protesting against the removal of the deposits. Infuriated by Jackson's easy triumph in the election, he conceived the idea of disciplining the people. He would show his claws; he would punish the people. He began the reduction of discounts, the collection of all balances against the state banks, and most disastrous of all, the refusal of credits to business men. Factories closed because they were unable to get loans, and workers were thrown into the street. Business houses began to fail because they could not get credit. And Biddle was delighted. He wrote jubilantly after a visit to New York and Washington that only the distress of the people would force a recharter of the bank, and he gloried in the suffering.

That which Jefferson had foreseen had come to pass. A moneyed institution was serving notice of its power to penalize the people who ignored its mandates, notice that it had power to dictate legislation to serve its monopolistic ends. Biddle arranged mass meetings of his cohorts to protest the removal of the deposits, and he inspired memorials to Congress. The orators of the bank, led by Clay and supported by Webster and Calhoun, were shedding tears in bathetic speeches and wiping their eyes on the public.

It was then that Clay introduced his resolution in the Senate censuring the President of the United States who refused to do the bidding of Biddle. It was play acting at its best. The galleries had been packed with the friends of the bank, and, in a long speech trembling with compassion for the suffering people, Clay appealed to Van Buren, presiding in the chair, to plead with Jackson for the hungry and starving. But Van Buren was as consummate an actor as Clay. He sat apparently intent on treasuring in his memory all that Clay had asked him to say. When Clay sank into his seat worn by his exertion and torn by his compassion for the people, every one turned to the suave Van Buren. Calling a Senator to the chair, he descended the rostrum, every eye in the Senate on him, and, walking to the seat of Clay, he bowed in his Chesterfieldian manner and gravely requested a pinch of the orator's snuff. Taken by surprise, Clay offered his snuff box. Van Buren opened it deliberately in the dramatic silence of the chamber, and extracting a pinch of snuff he applied it to his nostrils. Deliberately he closed the box, bowed again in his courtly fashion, and slowly returned to the rostrum. It was an anticlimax and the tears that Clay had shed had been dried in the sunshine of the smiles, and his appeal was lost in the tumult of the laughter.

Time was now running against the bank. Memorials against it were pouring in that had not been bought. Most disturbing of all were the memorials of state legislatures; but the climax came in the action of Governor Wolf of Pennsylvania, an erstwhile supporter, who turned upon his former friends with a denunciation of the bank as responsible for the depression.

The bitter debate on the resolution of censure, supported angrily by Clay, Webster, and Calhoun, ended in its adoption, the first act of the kind in American history. Years would pass before another such insult to a President would be offered to Andrew Johnson, pilloried for the crime of battling for the constitutional rights of the South and the preservation of its civilization.

But the censure of Andrew Jackson at the behest of the bank aroused the anger of the nation. The Jacksonians never failed accurately to appraise the feeling of the people. They momentarily confined themselves to the demand that the Clay resolution of censure with the vote of each Senator should be sent to the governor of each state for transmission to his legislature. No longer could there be any doubt that the bank could create a panic and depression, could punish the people for legislation it disliked, and if permitted to continue could ultimately dictate the legislation of the future.

Meanwhile, Clay, having failed to march to the presidency over a pavement of gold laid with the money of the bank, was losing interest. He who had involved Biddle in a losing struggle was becoming impatient with his importunities and complaints. The bank held on precariously for a time under the laws of Pennsylvania and then went down in a crash. Biddle retired to his countryseat to meditate on his blunders, and when he died, William Cullen Bryant of the New York *Evening Post* wrote that he had "died at his countryseat where he passed his last days in elegant retirement, which, if justice had been done, would have been spent in the penitentiary."

Jackson had won, but the censure rankled; and, in the closing days of the Jackson tenure in the White House, the Jacksonians, under the leadership of Benton, moved to have the censure stricken from the journal. Clay, Webster, and Calhoun made mournful speeches with Clay appearing for the occasion dressed in funereal black. In Benton's room the tables groaned under the weight of hams, turkeys, and whiskey for the refreshment of the faithful. The roll was called and the censure of one of the greatest of Americans was erased from the record in the presence of the Senators who had offered the insult.

Jackson's war on a moneyed monopoly that was presuming to dictate to the nation was his greatest service to the people. It put democracy on an even keel. It served notice that ours is a government by men and not by money. It asserted and maintained the preeminence of the people's government in the affairs of the country. It made good the Jeffersonian formula of equal rights with special privileges for none. And the arrogant plutocracy that had dared challenge the national government of all the people was buried in the grave of the national bank.

VIII

These were Jackson's three supreme achievements for Americanism. He had asserted with decision that we are a nation and that the Federal Union must be preserved. He had served notice that no nation can play fast and loose with treaties with the United States and had raised our national prestige to heights it had not known before. He had made good his assertion that the elected government of the republic is supreme and beyond the dictation of any group, however powerful, and that has not been successfully challenged from that day to this.

He who made that record is one of America's immortals.

But what a struggle! His foes were powerful. For eight years he faced and fought the most brilliant, eloquent, and resourceful leaders of the Senate—Clay, Webster, and Calhoun. Each of these had a large devoted following; each was unsurpassed, if ever equalled, in eloquence by any other trio in our history; each, though sometimes diverted by the rainbow chase of the presidency, was a lover of his country according to his light; and each was superlatively great. Jackson faced and fought and felled them all. He deserved to win by virtue of the right, but other men, equally right, would almost certainly have failed before such opposition. Thrice armed with the justice of his cause, he won because of the superb fighting heart within him and because of the unyielding determination that won the heart of America when he battled against the conquerors of Napoleon and wiped out the humiliations of the War of 1812 from behind the cotton bales of New Orleans.

And now the reign of Andrew Jackson was drawing to a close. Throughout his eight years in the White House he had fought his bitter battles under the handicap of ill health, and toward the end he was seriously ill though never for a moment had he made complaint, and every moment he was fighting. Toward the close he directed the struggle from a sickbed, propped up with pillows. Less than two weeks before he turned over the government to a successor of his choice, he celebrated Washington's birthday with a reception when too ill to stand, and he received his guests seated in the Blue Room, his figure bowed with weakness and care. He looked forward with delight to his return to the Hermitage where clustered sentimental memories. There on the grounds slept his wife, Rachel. He packed his belongings and prepared to leave the scene of his struggles. The Bible of Rachel which he had daily read and her portrait that stood upon the table were to return with him to his home in Tennessee.

In his last days in the White House he wrote his farewell to the American people. But his clear vision did not deceive him as to the dangers that loomed ahead. He clearly envisioned the coming years and he sorrowed over the picture he foresaw of Americans divided against themselves on the battlefields that would take a tragic toll of the most gallant youths of the nation. Though debilitated by disease and age, he dragged himself to the inauguration of his successor, sitting during the ceremony with bowed frame; and he sensed, as all knew, that the reverence of the multitude was for the setting rather than the rising sun, and that the cheers were for him. Benton, looking upon the scene and listening to the ovation, observed that the cheers were "the acclaim of posterity breaking from the bosom of contemporaries." Too weak to do more than acknowledge the ovation with a mute sign, he raised his hand.

That night he slept in the White House on the insistence of Van Buren who urged him to remain until May or June when the journey home would be more comfortable. But he was homesick for Tennessee and the home that held so many tender memories. The next day he walked across the street to the Blair House to bid farewell to faithful friends who had won honorable scars in his service. And here the old fighting spirit flared again when he said that his sole regret was that he had been unable to shoot Clay and hang Calhoun. He was sorry that the problem of Texas had not been solved; he said that the Oregon dispute should be settled at fifty-four forty; but of all things, he said, "never once take your eyes off Texas."

The next day he began his journey home receiving ovations on the way. There at the Hermitage he was to live for several years in intimate touch with national affairs, actively advising succeeding Presidents. Then came the closing scene. With his grim determination he even held death back to bid farewell to his friends and Negro servants. He thanked them and expressed the hope that he might meet them again in heaven. And then he closed his eyes. The great drama was finished. And thus passed to eternity one of the greatest fighting figures in all the tide of time.